BR
in

BAe 146 in Europe

Leo Marriott

3

FROM THE
FLIGHTDECK

LONDON

IAN ALLAN LTD

Acknowledgements

This book has been written with the wholehearted and enthusiastic co-operation of Dan-Air, and I would like to place on record the names of all those concerned.

Pauline Kirkman, assistant Public Relations Officer with the airline, was responsible for making the arrangements to carry out the necessary flights. Captain Larry Buist, BAe146 Fleet Manager, kindly gave permission for me to have access to the flightdeck of the aircraft concerned, and gave his willing blessing to the project.

Bob Willis and Mike Forsyth looked after me during an extremely interesting visit to the airline's operations section at Gatwick (and a well known pub nearby!) At Newcastle the station manager, Steve Casey, helped to smooth my path on several occasions.

The most vital help, of course, came from the pilots with whom I was fortunate enough to fly; without exception, they were only too willing to answer questions and provide information. With patient forbearance, they tolerated me peering over their shoulders, camera clicking and tape recorder running. Several were subsequently able to read the draft manuscript and correct some of my worst mistakes.

From outside the airline, help was forthcoming in the provision of photographs and charts. I would particularly like to thank Derek Hodgson of British Airways AERAD Chart

First published 1987

ISBN 0 7110 1732 8

Published by Ian Allan Ltd, Shepperton, Surrey; and printed by Ian Allan Printing Ltd at their works at Coombelands in Runnymede, England

Department who provided the facilities to reprint the various maps and charts in this book.

The Civil Aviation Authority provided photographs of Air Traffic Control (ATC) installations and gave permission for information from their various publications to be reproduced; this was arranged through Peter Kennedy of their Public Relations Department.

Author's Note: Aviation is a constantly changing world and consequently some of the procedures outlined in this book have been amended or cancelled. The reporting Point RIBEL, mentioned in the early part of the book, has been withdrawn, as has the Barton VOR. Aircraft departing Newcastle now route directly to Pole Hill. Similarly, there have been some changes to the Dan-Air Schedules for 1987 and the aircraft from Newcastle now routes to Bergen via Stavanger, returning direct. The flight numbers have been amended accordingly.

Cover:
BAe 146 of Dan-Air seen at Newcastle Airport in summer 1987. *Dan-Air*

Introduction

Every weekday morning during the summer, a BAe146-100 airliner operated by Dan-Air lifts off from Newcastle Airport in the Northeast of England and heads south for London-Gatwick. By 2000hr the aircraft will have operated two complete return flights between Newcastle and London, as well as a round trip from Newcastle to Bergen and Stavanger in Norway. These flights form part of the extensive schedule service network in the UK and Europe operated by Dan-Air, an airline perhaps better known to many people for its activities in the holiday charter flight market. However, the expanding scheduled services form a substantial part of the airline's activities and the three BAe146 aircraft presently flying for Dan-Air make a significant contribution to this network. Indeed, the airline was the first operator of the type and has since maintained a close relationship with British Aerospace.

The Newcastle-based aircraft returns home in the evening where routine checks and maintenance are carried out overnight to ready it for the next day's programme. However, this is summertime and at weekends the emphasis changes to the charter market; the aircraft is despatched to Tees-side Airport on the Friday evening to operate a series of charter flights from there to Spain, Italy and the Channel Islands. Thus, on a typical Friday the aircraft will be almost continuously in use; during the 24hr period commencing at 0700hr it will operate no less than 10 separate flights covering a total distance of around 4,000 miles, landing at six different airports in three separate countries. More significantly it will have generated 350,880 revenue-earning passenger miles, using perhaps 20% less fuel than its immediate predecessor, the BAC One-Eleven.

The full timetable for the aircraft on a typical Friday is shown in the accompanying table, and the operation of the aircraft during the ensuing 24hr is described in the following pages. Although the period covered by this book is set in the summer, it should not be forgotten that the scheduled services described are a permanent commitment, forming a considerable challenge to the aircraft, its aircrews and the airline. An unserviceability can delay the aircraft and have a knock-on effect on the rest of the day's flights. The weather in Europe can create considerable problems at all times of the year, and during the winter additional hazards caused by ice and snow must be overcome. The relatively short sectors impose high workload demands on the pilots with constant climbs and descents in busy sections of airspace, and relatively little time spent in a relaxing cruise at altitudes above the weather.

It is also important to remember the part played by the people on the ground in the successful completion of any flight. There are, of course, the engineers who toil to keep the aircraft airworthy and safe to fly, the airline operations staff who ensure that the aircraft is properly loaded and monitor the progress of the flight so that the necessary passenger-handling arrangements can be made at the various airports along the route; and finally there is the worldwide air traffic control network which ensures the safety of the aircraft in flight, and guides it down to a

Above right:
The BAe146 presents a unique profile amongst modern airliners with its upswept tail, high wing and four underslung engines. *All photographs by the author unless otherwise credited*

landing at the destination. Although this book is concerned with the view 'from the flight-deck', it is intended to give some insight into the other side of the picture as the flight progresses.

As an airline pilot, you quickly learn that the week is not made up of five working days and a pleasant relaxing weekend; nor does the day start and end at reasonable hours. Thus, the Captain's day begins early in the morning with the insistent bleep of an alarm clock at 0515. Thirty minutes later he is in his car, driving from a quiet Northumbrian village to Newcastle's busy international airport . . .

Schedule of flights for the Newcastle-based BAe146 (Friday)

From	To	Flt No	STD	STA	Dist	Time
Newcastle	Gatwick	DA101	0700	0810	300	50min
Gatwick	Newcastle	DA102	0850	1000	300	50min
Newcastle	Bergen	DA846	1040	1155	400	1hr 15min
Bergen	Stavanger	DA846	1225	1255	100	20min
Stavanger	Newcastle	DA846	1315	1530	350	1hr 5min
Newcastle	Gatwick	DA107	1700	1810	300	50min
Gatwick	Newcastle	DA108	1850	2000	300	50min
Newcastle	Teesside	DA2852P	2230	2245	30	10min
Teesside	Palma	DA2852	2355	0245	1,000	2hr 45min
Palma	Teesside	DA2853	0330	0630	1,000	2hr 45min

Total distance travelled: 4,080 nautical miles
Total time en route: 11hr 40min
Notes: All times are given in British Summer Time. Local times will vary and one hour should be subtracted to give UTC/GMT. Distances are approximate. The time en route for each sector given in the right-hand column are typical airborne times. The scheduled times of arrival and departure add on a time allowance to cover start-up, taxying and parking, as well as minor operational delays.

Key to Cockpit Layout

A	NAV1 frequency selector
B	Autopilot mode control
C	NAV course selector
D	Autopilot altitude selector
E	NAV2 frequency selector
F	Autopilot mode annunciator
G	Undercarriage lever
H	Engine oil pressure and temperature
I	Engine N1 gauge
K	Engine turbine gas temperature
L	Engine N2 gauge
M	Fuel flowmeter
N	Fuel quantity gauge
O	Attitude director indicator
P	Airspeed indicator
Q	Altimeter
R	Standby artificial horizon
S	Digital clock/stopwatch
T	Radio magnetic indicator (RMI)
U	Horizontal situation display
V	Vertical speed indicator
W	Standby altimeter
X	Flap position indicator
Y	Brake pressures
Z	Cabin pressure gauge
AA	ADF frequency selectors
BB	VHF communication frequency selectors
CC	Transponder
SB	Station box
MWS	Master warning system
TMS	Thrust management system

Above:
General view of the flightdeck.

Below:
Drawing of cockpit layout.

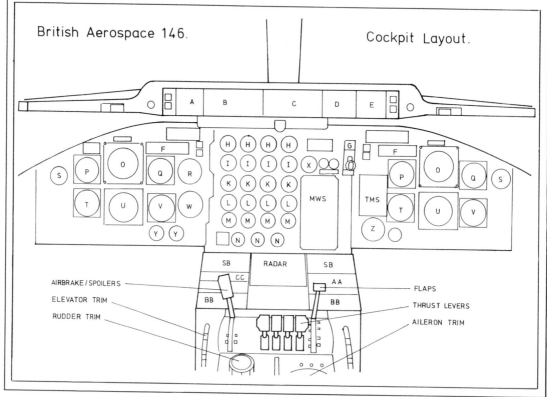

British Aerospace 146.   Cockpit Layout.

AIRBRAKE / SPOILERS
ELEVATOR TRIM
RUDDER TRIM

FLAPS
THRUST LEVERS
AILERON TRIM

Glossary and Abbreviations

ADF Automatic Direction Finder — aircraft equipment which displays bearings of transmissions from ground-based medium frequency radio beacons

ADI Attitude Director Indicator — one of the primary flight instruments based on the artificial horizon

ADT Approved Departure Time

Airway A corridor of airspace between specified altitudes and normally 10 miles wide. The route is usually defined by radio navigation aids; upper airways are above Flight Level 250

ALT Altitude (autopilot mode)

APU Auxiliary Power Unit

ASI Airspeed Indicator

ATC Air Traffic Control

ATCC Air Traffic Control Centre

ATIS Automatic Terminal Information Service — a continuous radio transmission giving weather and landing information at an airport

AUW All-up Weight

BAe British Aerospace

BP British Petroleum

BR British Caledonian (callsign abbreviation)

BST British Summer Time

C Centigrade or Celsius

C of G Centre of Gravity

DA Dan-Air (callsign abbreviation)

FIR Flight Information Region — the basic division of airspace for ATC purposes. Each FIR is operationally administered by ATCC

Flight Level The altitude shown at 500ft intervals by an altimeter when set to a reference atmospheric pressure of 1013mb. Use of this system assists ATC by ensuring that all aircraft are using a common reference system for altitude reporting

fpm Feet Per Minute

GMT Greenwich Mean Time

GPU Ground Power Unit

GSL Glideslope (autopilot mode)

HDG Heading (autopilot mode)

HP High Pressure

hr Hour

HSD Horizontal Situation Display

IAS Indicated Airspeed

ILS Instrument Landing System

kg Kilogrammes

kHz Kilohertz

LATCC London Air Traffic Control Centre

LNAV Localiser/Navigation (autopilot mode)

mb Millibars

MHz Megahertz

MWS Master Warning System

NAV Navigation Set, for receiving signals from ground-based VHF navigation aids

NDB Non-Directional Beacon — a medium-frequency ground-based radio navigation aid

NOSIG Term used in weather reports to indicate that no significant change in the reported conditions is expected in the next 30min

NOTAM Notice to Airmen

N1 Rotational speed of the first stage fan on a turbofan engine, expressed as a percentage of the nominal maximum

N2 Rotational speed of the first stage turbine in the engine, expressed as a percentage of the nominal maximum

OKTA Term used in weather reports to indicate one-eighth of the sky area when determining the extent of a cloud layer

PA Public Announcement System

RTF Radio Telephone

QFE Code term indicating the reported air pressure at a specific point, normally above sea level. Using QFE as a reference, an altimeter will show height above the specified point

QNH Code term indicating the reported sea level air pressure at a particular point. Using this as a reference, an altimeter will show altitude above sea level

SID Standard Instrument Departure

Squawk A four-figure code allocated by ATC which, when set on an aircraft's transponder, will be repeated on ground-based radar displays to assist identification and tracking of the flight

STA Scheduled Time of Arrival

STAR Standard Arrival Route

STD Scheduled Time of Departure

TAS True Airspeed

TGT Turbine Gas Temperature

TMA Terminal Control Area

TMS Thrust Management System
UTC Universal Co-ordinated Time — a standard aviation time system used on a worldwide basis. In effect, it is just another name for GMT
VHF Very High Frequency
V/L VOR or Localiser (autopilot mode)
VOR VHF Omni-Directional Radio Range — a ground-based radio navigation aid which transmits extremely accurate bearings or radials around the full 360° of the compass
VR Speed at which the aircraft is rotated into the flying attitude during a take-off run
V ref Target speed over the runway threshold when landing
VS Vertical Speed (autopilot mode)
VSI Vertical Speed Indicator
V1 Speed above which a take-off run will be continued in the event of the failure of a power unit — sometimes referred to as the Decision Speed
V2 Safe climb-out speed following the loss of a power unit

'Eight four six is passing the marker.' The ILS Glideslope aerial is in the foreground.

DAYBREAK . . .

Captain Peter Hertzberg arrives at Newcastle Airport just before 0600 (BST). One advantage of an early start is that at least there is plenty of room in the staff car park — a small consolation for being up and about when most of the world is still sleeping. At this time of the year the sun has already been up for a couple of hours, and it is a clear morning with a light breeze and little cloud. Leaving the car, he proceeds immediately to the Dan-Air traffic office on the first floor of the passenger terminal building where he checks which aircraft is scheduled for the Dan-Air Flight 101 to Gatwick. Today it is 'Golf Bravo Kilo Mike November' (G-BKMN), the second of two BAe146s delivered direct from the manufacturers to the airline. Dan-Air's third machine was one of two originally used by the RAF prior to placing an order for two aircraft to be used by the Queen's Flight.

The Captain can also find out from the roster board who his co-pilot will be today, although in practice he will probably already be aware of this. To operate the single BAe146 from Newcastle the airline has six Captains and six co-pilots based there; each is provided with a duty roster showing which flights he will be operating for a period of a month ahead, and a two-pilot crew will often work together for several days in a row. The responsibility for planning the crewing requirements lies with the airline's operations department at their main base at Gatwick Airport; altogether there are 32 pilots in the BAe146 fleet.

Before leaving the traffic office the Captain will pick up an envelope containing the Captain's Briefing, advising him of the route and scheduled times of the flights for which he will be responsible. It will also give him the names of the handling agents for the flight at each airport it will visit, together with telephone and telex numbers and codes of these and other relevant agencies. On a flight to Gatwick this information is not particularly vital as the aircraft will be handled by the company at all times, but this is not always the case. Finally, the brief will contain any special information which should be brought to the

Left:
Captain Hertzberg and his First Officer work out the fuel requirements for the flight to Gatwick.

11

Above:
The flight planning office is below the control tower at Newcastle Airport.

which include synoptic charts showing the actual weather situation and high level charts showing the winds at various altitudes.

The crew will also check the NOTAMS (Notices to Airmen) which will advise of any unserviceability or change in status of any navigation aid or facility which they may intend to use. These come in two forms: Class I which come off the teleprinter via the AFTN and usually relate to very recent or short-term occurrences, and Class II which take the form of a published bulletin sent by post to every airfield and summarising the NOTAMS and navigation warnings in force at the date of sending. These are available for the crew to collect and take with them to the aircraft. Today there are no significant problems, although one NOTAM refers to one of the runway access taxiways being closed at Gatwick for surface repairs. This apparently routine information will cause a minor incident later in the day.

The weather forecasts are all good, both for Gatwick and the nominated diversion airfields (Heathrow, Luton and Bournemouth), and so interest centres on the projected winds at cruising altitude of Flight Level (FL) 270. These are generally from the northwest, and averaging 60kt, which represents a useful tailwind and will save some 5min flying time overall on the southbound trip, but will add a similar amount to the northbound leg later in the morning.

Armed with the basic information provided by the briefing staff, the crew now concentrate on the navigation and fuel log; this is a standard *pro forma* which is drawn up by the airlines operations staff. On one side is listed the basic route of the flight, together with information on the identification and frequencies of the various radio navigation aids to be used. The distance of each leg and the elapsed time of each leg at standard speeds assuming nil winds is also listed. Having calculated the wind vector for each leg, the time can be amended as necessary and the total time en route calculated. The other side of the form is concerned with fuel calculations, a matter of some importance. Having calculated the flight time for the route, the amount of fuel required for this can be calculated or read off from tables. To this basic figure are added allowances for taxying and start-up, holding in the air for 30min and flight to the alternative airfield from the original destination if a diversion is necessary. A 5% allowance is added to all flight times to give a margin for increased fuel consumption, perhaps due to winds different to the forecast (a not unknown

Captain's notice, such as the presence of a VIP on board or, perhaps, some unusual cargo which may require special attention.

Leaving the terminal building, he walks the short distance to the aircrew flight briefing office in the operations building below the control tower. Here he meets Andy Mathesson, his co-pilot for the morning, who has already been busy collecting the meteorological information necessary for planning the flight. Although Newcastle, in common with many airports, does not have its own meteorological forecasting office, it can obtain all the required data for the UK and Europe by means of two teleprinter networks, the AFTN (Aeronautical Fixed Telecommunications Network) and MOTNE (Meteorological Operational Teleprinter Network, Europe). The former will provide, on request, en route and area forecasts while the latter has a continuous transmission of airfield actual weather reports and TAFs (Terminal Area Forecasts) for virtually all UK and major European airports. The relevant information is photocopied and handed to the pilot together with copies of the various charts occurrence). For the flight to Gatwick in today's conditions, the total requirement comes to 3,310kg but this, of course, is a minimum and the Captain has complete discretion to carry more fuel if he sees fit. In the winter, when Gatwick is notoriously prone to long periods of fog in the early morning, it is often prudent to carry enough fuel for up to 2hr holding which would add another 3,000kg to the uptake. After a brief discussion, the Captain decides to uplift a total of 4,300kg; the First Officer passes this figure by telephone to the traffic office who contact the refuelling company (BP) and request them to refuel the aircraft to that figure.

With the paperwork complete for the moment, there is time for a quick chat with another Dan-Air crew who are preparing for a scheduled flight to Amsterdam aboard a BAC One-Eleven, before leaving the flight planning office and walking across the apron to the aircraft which is parked on Stand 8. It is now 0625 local time, there is a bustle of activity around the aircraft as the pilots walk up the steps and drop their bags in the spaces behind the seat on the flightdeck. The cabin crew are busy stowing the hot meals in the galley which is situated immediately behind the flightdeck, forming an entry lobby by the forward main door. The refuelling bowser has arrived and the operator is connecting the fuel line to the pressure fuelling point set into the leading edge of the starboard wing. The First Officer goes to conduct an external inspection of the aircraft and to supervise the refuelling, while the Captain confers with the Engineer who has already carried out a full daily check during the previous couple of hours. The aircraft's technical log is produced and one or two minor points are discussed before the Captain signs as accepting the aircraft fit for the flight. There are one or two minor unserviceabilities: for

Above:
The Captain consults the departure charts to check the initial routeing after take-off.

example, the No 1 Engine Fuel Flowmeter readout of fuel consumed is not working and there is a malfunctioning light on the engine Thrust Management System (TMS) control panel. However, this level of mechanical problems causes no difficulty and rectification can be deferred until the aircraft is due for a scheduled check.

In the meantime, the First Officer has completed his external check of the aircraft and the fuel uplift has been completed. As he settles down in the right-hand seat on the flightdeck, the Engineer leaves and is replaced by the Dispatcher from the airline's traffic department who is responsible for preparing the aircraft's load sheet. This form is laid out so that the passenger and baggage load, together with fuel carried, can be displayed and weight and balance calculations carried out.

Below:
'Mike November' stands on the apron at Newcastle with steps in place, ready to board the passengers.

Passenger check-in will have commenced an hour ago up in the departure hall of the terminal. Each passenger has their luggage weighed and is categorised as male, female, child or infant. Standard weights are allowed for each (male 78kg, female 68kg, child 43kg, infant 10kg) and seat allocation is made within one of four bays in the cabin to preserve a rough balance. Check-in should be completed 20min before departure and at that time the figures for passengers and baggage weights are passed by radio to the dispatcher at the aircraft. On this occasion the final load is 48 males, eight females, two children and 250kg of baggage to be stowed in the holds. Including the 4,300kg of fuel, the take-off weight is now at 31,143kg which is comfortably within the maximum allowed of just over 38,000kg. Allowing for the calculated fuel-burn of 1,700kg, the landing weight should be 29,443kg — again well within the maximum permitted. Finally, the balance calculations are carried out using the graphs on the load sheet; there is a moment's apprehension as the aircraft's C of G is shown to be just outside the permitted range, giving rise to the possibility that some passengers will have to be moved forward in the cabin in order to correct matters. However, a check shows an error in entering the data on the sheet and, once this has been corrected, the balance works out within limits — even allowing for an extra passenger who has checked in late and whose details have been passed to the dispatcher on the radio as she works on the flightdeck.

With the aircraft's weight finalised, the First Officer takes a flipleaf card booklet which shows the operating speeds for take-off and landing at various weights in increments of 1,000kg. The figure of 31,000kg is selected as the nearest approximation to the take-off weight and the card is clipped to the instrument panel, just to the right of the Master Warning System (MWS) display panel. The speeds shown are then marked on the airspeed indicators by means of coloured plastic pointers or 'bugs' set into the rim of the instrument. Having set his own, the First Officer calls out the figures to the Captain who also sets up his ASI. The important speeds are V1, the speed at which a take-off will be continued even if a power unit should fail after that point; VR, the take-off speed at which the aircraft is rotated into the flying attitude by easing back the control column; V2, which is the safe climb-out speed in the event of losing an engine during or after take-off.

With less than 15min to go before the scheduled departure time, the passengers are boarding the aircraft by both the front and rear doors. While this is happening the First Officer switches on the VHF radios, two of which are carried, and selects both to 119.7MHz which is Newcastle Tower's frequency. Selecting VHF1 on the station box set into the forward end of the centre console, he presses the transmit switch on the control column and makes the first RTF call of the day.

First Officer: 'Newcastle Tower, this is Dan-Air one zero one, radio check on Box One.'

Newcastle Tower: 'Dan-Air one zero one, Newcastle, reading you strength five.'

Having established that this VHF set is functioning correctly, he selects VHF2 and makes another call.

First Officer: 'Newcastle Tower, this is Dan-Air one zero one on Box Two for the data.'

Newcastle Tower: 'Roger one zero one. Runway is two five, surface wind two eight zero degrees at one two knots, QNH is one zero two one, QFE touchdown runway two five is one zero one two, temperature plus niner, Time Check zero five four six.'

The First Officer acknowledges these figures and transfers the pressure settings (QNH and QFE) to the altimeters. With one instrument set to QNH and reading altitude above sea level, and the other to QFE and reading height above the airfield (zero feet at the moment), then the difference in reading between the two should equal the airfield elevation. This gives a useful check that both are functioning correctly.

The next job is to sort out the maps and charts required for the departure and en route phases of the flight. Every commercial airliner carries a considerable amount of documentation, known as the 'ship's library', which will include such items as the technical log, handling notes, performance data charts, check lists and charts. Arrival and departure information for various airfields is contained on A5-size charts contained in a loose-leaf binder, and the First Officer selects the appropriate Newcastle Departure Procedures Chart from the file and clips it to his control column. He also makes sure that the en route charts EUR/1 and H108/109 are to hand. Captain and First Officer study the departure chart which specifies the noise abatement routine to be followed after departure from Runway 25. In this case the aircraft is to climb

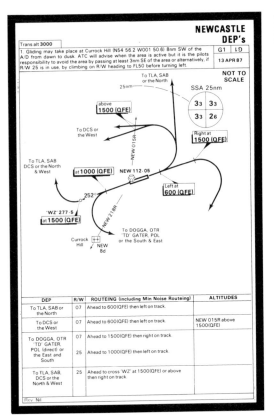

NEWCASTLE
DEP's

Trans alt 3000

1. Gliding may take place at Currock Hill (N54 56.2 W001 50.6) 8nm SW of the A/D from dawn to dusk. ATC will advise when the area is active but it is the pilots responsibility to avoid the area by passing at least 3nm SE of the area or alternatively, if R/W 25 is in use, by climbing on R/W heading to FL50 before turning left.

G1 L9

13 APR 87

NOT TO SCALE

To TLA, SAB
or the North

SSA 25nm

25nm

above
1500 (QFE)

To DCS or
the West

NEW 015R

33 33

33 26

Right at
1500 (QFE)

To TLA, SAB
DCS or the North
& West

at **1000 (QFE)**   NEW 112·05

Left at
600 (QFE)

252°

NEW 218R

'WZ' 277·5
at **1500 (QFE)**

To DOGGA, OTR
'TD' GATER, POL
or the South & East

Currock
Hill   ++   NEW
8d

DEP	R/W	ROUTEING (including Min Noise Routeing)	ALTITUDES
To TLA, SAB or the North	07	Ahead to 600(QFE) then left on track.	
To DCS or the West	07	Ahead to 600(QFE) then left on track.	NEW 015R above 1500(QFE)
To DOGGA, OTR 'TD' GATER, POL (direct) or the East and South	07	Ahead to 1500(QFE) then right on track.	
	25	Ahead to 1000(QFE) then left on track.	
To TLA, SAB, DCS or the North & West	25	Ahead to cross 'WZ' at 1500(QFE) or above then right on track.	

Rev. Nil.

Left:
Chart showing routes for Newcastle Departures. *AERAD*

straight ahead after take-off until passing 1,000ft on the QFE before turning left on course to the southwest.

Once airborne the route will take the aircraft over the Pennines, joining the airways system at a point called RIBEL which is just north of Leeds. It will then cross the Barton VOR just west of Manchester before turning left on to a track of approximately 160° and following Airway Amber One overhead Birmingham, then passing to the west of Heathrow on track to the Midhurst VOR in Sussex. From there it will turn east and follow the relevant approach procedure into Gatwick, although the exact inbound routeing will be passed to the aircraft by ATC after it is airborne.

With the last passengers boarding, the crew start running through the formal pre-start checklist. This is available in one of the manuals as a written list, but the main headings can be called up for display on the weather radar screen situated at the forward

Below:
The weather radar screen, set into the centre console, can also be used to display checklists.

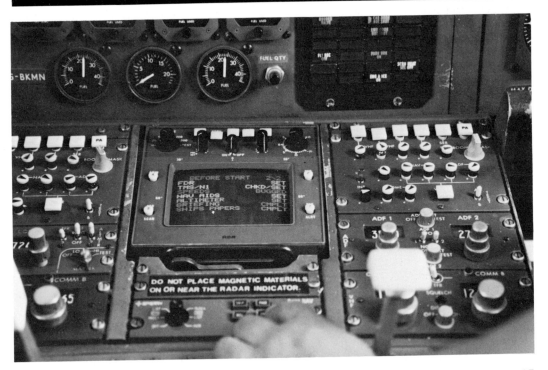

end of the centre console. This is colour-coded so that the item being checked appears in yellow on the list while items waiting to be checked are in green and those already done appear in blue. The system is simply controlled by push-buttons set into panels on the outer sides of the flightdeck. The First Officer runs through the checks, calling out each item in turn while the Captain carries out the appropriate action and reports.

The aircraft already has electrical power from the Garrett AiResearch GTCP36-100 APU situated in the tail, and which would have been started by the engineers well before the crew boarded the aircraft. The pre-start checks then run through the various systems such as brakes, hydraulics, fuel, pressurisation and anti-icing. The controls for all these are set in the overhead panel where they are accessible to both crew members. Further checks prepare the passenger cabin; signs are set and illuminated and the air conditioning is set up as required.

The fuel flowmeters are zeroed so that the fuel used is at zero on each gauge, and each is checked as reading nil flow. The fuel contents gauges are checked and show 2,100kg in the port tanks and 2,200kg in the starboard side; this agrees with the total of 4,300kg which was uplifted.

To prolong engine life, and for noise abatement purposes, most jet airliners do not employ full power for take-off. Instead, a suitable power setting is selected from performance tables which takes into account the aircraft's weight, runway length, climb-out profiles and weather conditions (temperature and wind). On the BAe146 this is given as a percentage of maximum fanspeed on the Avco Lycoming ALF502R-5 turbofans, a figure expressed as N1. Other engine parameters, which are displayed in four columns of instruments in the centre of the main panel, include N2, TGT and fuel flow. These are, respectively, the percentage speed of the engine core shaft, the Turbine Gas Temperature and the Fuel Flow Rate shown in kg/hr. Although the engines are controlled by conventional throttle levers in the central console, many engine functions can be preset and controlled automatically by the Thrust Management System. Although not a full autothrottle system, it can take care of

Below:
The cockpit overhead panel — from left to right are the controls for the fuel system, electrical supplies, APU and engine starting, cabin pressurisation and air supply, airframe and engine anti-icing.

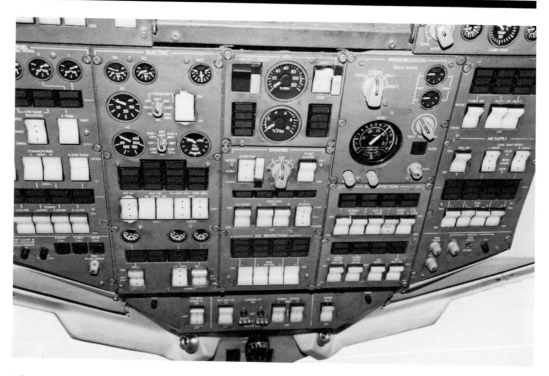

synchronisation of the engines (an important chore as the fans can produce some irritating resonances if not correctly synchronised) and control engine parameters to set limits. In preparation for take-off, the required 91% N1 setting is set up on the instruments using a knurled knob on each to position the 'bug'. The take-off speeds are rechecked and the ASI setting confirmed, together with the required flap setting (18°) for take-off.

On short-haul routes in the UK and Europe, most commercial aircraft rely on the standard combination of VOR/DME and ADF for en route navigation. The former will give a readout of bearing and distance from the selected ground station, and will also define a radial along which the aircraft can be steered in order to overfly the facility. ADF, otherwise known as a radio compass, will indicate the direction of the radio beacon selected relative to the heading of the aircraft. It works on medium range broadcast frequencies and is considerably less accurate and reliable than the more modern VOR/DME combination. As part of the pre-start checks the co-pilot, with the agreement of the Captain, selects the frequencies of the first two VORs to be used after take-off. The selector controls are mounted along the top edge of the glareshield and he turns the rotary knobs until 112.4MHz shows on NAV1 and 113.5MHz on NAV2, these being the Barton and Newcastle VORs respectively. Tuning to a VOR frequency also selects the allocated DME installation automatically. On the Horizontal Situation Display in front of each pilot, the green NAV2 needle swings to the correct bearing and the DME read-out immediately above shows 0.5 miles. In addition, the First Officer checks the aural coding by selecting NAV2 on his station box and listening for the letters NEW in Morse code which confirm that the correct VOR is selected.

It is normal procedure for one pilot to actually fly and operate the aircraft while being monitored by the other pilot, who is also responsible for all communications with Air Traffic Control. They are respectively designated as Handling and Monitoring pilots and today it has been agreed that Andy will be the Handling pilot on the flight to Gatwick. On the return leg, the roles will be reversed. As Handling pilot, Andy gives a departure briefing which covers the engine and speed settings, noise abatement routine and climb-out procedure. He also runs through the actions to be carried out in the event of an engine failure during or after the take-off.

Once the briefing is completed, the No 1 stewardess comes forward to confirm a total of 58 passengers are now on board and that the groundcrew are ready to remove the steps. The Captain checks the figures with the Dispatcher and signs the load sheet and the passenger and cargo manifests. He tears off the top copies which are retained aboard the aircraft and hands the rest to the Dispatcher who bids them a cheerful farewell and hurries down the steps which are then promptly pulled away. The cabin staff close the front and rear doors and confirm to the flightdeck that both are secured.

As the pre-start formalities are completed, the Captain presses his transmit switch and calls for start-up clearance:

Captain: 'Newcastle Tower, Dan-Air one zero one is ready for start.'
Newcastle Tower: 'Dan-Air one zero one, pushback and start approved, temperature plus nine.'

The request for start-up is a formality on this occasion as there are no delays for aircraft operating into Gatwick this morning. However, it can be a different story at times during the winter when thick fog may cause a build-up of traffic waiting to land at Gatwick or Heathrow. In such cases London Air Traffic Control Centre (LATCC) may decide that it is better to hold aircraft on the ground at their departure airfield in order to reduce congestion in the London TMA, and also to enable airline operators to save on fuel costs. In such cases ATC at the departure airfield would advise the Captain of the delay together with an Approved Departure Time (ADT or 'slot'). However, there are no such problems today and the First Officer now calls up the Ground Engineer who is standing by the nose of the aircraft wearing a headset which is plugged into the aircraft's intercom by means of an external socket.

First Officer: 'Hello Engineer, we are all closed up and ready to start. We have been cleared for pushback and are ready to go.'

The Engineer has already checked that the baggage hold doors have been correctly closed and secured, and he now takes a quick look behind the aircraft to check that all is clear before motioning to the tug driver to start the pushback. The aircraft is parked on Stand 8 facing the pier and the holding lounges, so it is necessary to move the aircraft backwards and turn it through 90° so that it will end up parallel to the pier and facing in the right direction to taxi towards the runway. For this purpose a tug is connected to the aircraft's nosewheel by means of a drawbar so that the tractor can also steer the aircraft.

With a slight lurch, the 146 starts to move backwards and the First Officer begins to run through the starting procedures. The controls for this are all positioned on the overhead panel where he selects the Start Master Switch to 'on' and turns the Rotary Engine Selector Switch to '4', ready to start the starboard outer power unit. While this is going on, the Captain speaks to the passengers for the first time by means of the cabin PA system which he can select on his station box.

Captain: 'Good morning ladies and gentlemen, this is Captain Hertzberg speaking and, on behalf of myself and my First Officer, Andy Mathesson, I would like to welcome you aboard this British Aerospace 146 for our flight to Gatwick this morning. We are just pushing back and will shortly be taxying out for a departure on the westerly runway. After take-off, we shall be turning left and climbing to an altitude of 27,000ft. Our route will take us to the west of Manchester before heading south over Birmingham and we expect to arrive at Gatwick on time, at ten past eight. The weather at Gatwick is fine, although it is a little cool with the temperature only 10°C. We hope that you will enjoy your flight and I will speak to you again when we are on our way.'

With the pushback complete, the First Officer goes ahead with starting the engines, pressing the engine start switch for one second with his right hand and resting his left hand on the

Below:
Pushback completed, the tractor pulls away, and the aircraft is ready to taxi.

Above:
The four thrust levers are set into the centre console, at the base of which are the rudder and aileron trims, and the parking brake.

No 4 thrust lever. As lights on the starter panel confirm that the engine is turning, and then that the ignitors are functioning, he moves the thrust lever forward to the ground idle position as the N2 gauge winds up through 10%. This movement opens the fuel feed cock and the engine continues to spool up until it settles at ground idle with N2 rpm at 50%, some 15 or 20sec after initiating the start. During the spool up, the TGT gauge is monitored to ensure that it does not read above the maximum permitted of 824°C, in which case the engine would be shut down immediately. With the engine running, the oil pressure is checked and then the Rotary Selector Switch is turned to No 3 for the procedure to be repeated, and then again for the other two.

With all four engines running, the TGTs settle down to read between 450°C and 500°C, N1 rpm at 25% and N2 at 50%, while each engine is consuming fuel at the rate of 150kg/hr. In winter the engine anti-icing system would be switched on at this stage but this is not necessary today and checks continue with the hydraulic and electrical systems. The former is pressurised by pumps on Nos 2 and 3 engines (yellow and green systems) to give a full capability in the event of failure of either engine. Fuel pumps are selected 'on', brake fans selected 'on', cockpit screen heaters 'on' and the cabin air selected.

While the start-up checks are completed, the ground engineer has been monitoring the engines externally and supervising the un-coupling of the towbar. The tractor pulls away to the right and the First Officer now calls him on the intercom.

First Officer: 'Thank you, Engineer, that was a good start and we are ready to go. We will see you clear on the right. Cheerio.'

The engineer gives a thumbs up signal in acknowledgement and, after disconnecting his headset jackplug, walks away to the right of the aircraft. A final check is made that the flightdeck windows are closed and that the MWS indicates that the cabin doors are all closed. The Captain calls on the radio for taxi clearance.

Captain: 'Newcastle Tower, Dan-Air one zero one is ready to taxi.'
Newcastle Tower: 'Dan-Air one zero one, taxi to holding point bravo for runway two five. The QNH is one zero two zero.'
Captain: 'Runway two five, one zero two zero, Dan-Air one zero one.'

Following a visual check to the left and right of the aircraft, the First Officer releases the brakes. Ground idle thrust is enough to make the aircraft move very slowly forward; he checks the operation of the brakes with the foot pedals before easing the thrust levers forward to taxi the aircraft off the parking apron, around the end of the pier towards the holding point short of the runway. The time is 0607 UTC (0707 local time) and pushback was initiated at 0604, so the whole procedure has taken less than 3min. While the aircraft is on the move, the litany of pre-take-off checks continues: flaps are selected and checked at the take-off setting at 18° and, as the aircraft turns to the left and then to the right on the taxiways, both pilots check their flight and

Above:
A glance down shows the cabin status prior to take-off.

navigation instruments for correct indications. Rudder and aileron trims are set to neutral, and the elevator trim is confirmed as set to the correct position for the aircraft's centre of gravity as calculated from the load and trim sheet.

As the 146 approaches the holding point, the checklist is interrupted by a call from ATC:

Newcastle Tower: 'Dan-Air one zero one is cleared to enter, backtrack, and line up runway two five. I have your departure instructions if you are ready to copy.'
Captain: 'Roger, one zero one is entering the runway to backtrack and we are ready to copy.'
Newcastle Tower: 'Dan-Air one zero one, after departure a left turn after noise abatement on track for Ribel, climbing to Flight Level two three zero. Squawk seven two three zero.'

While the aircraft has been taxying, the Aerodrome Controller in the Tower will have consulted his Approach Radar Controller situated in the Radar Room below the Visual Control Room. Approach will have formulated these departure instructions in order to ensure that the aircraft will be kept clear of other traffic flying in the area. The squawk refers to the code which the pilot will set on the aircraft's transponder, and these figures will show up on the radar display in order to identify the DA101. The Captain acknowledges the clearance and dials up 7230 on the transponder which is situated on the centre console immediately below his station box.

Due to the layout of the airfield at Newcastle, it is necessary for an aircraft using Runway 25 to taxi along almost the whole length of the runway before turning round and taking-off. This procedure is known as backtracking, and sometimes has to be carried out at the double if other aircraft are on finals to land! As the aircraft rumbles briskly down the runway the rest of the take-off checks are completed. The TMS is checked and the settings of the bugs on the gauges are confirmed, as are the ASI bugs for the various take-off speeds; settings of the radio navigation aids and transponder are also checked. In the case of the runway being very wet or covered with a combination of ice, snow or slush, continuous ignition is selected for the engines to prevent a flame-out if large quantities of water are ingested during the take-off run.

As the aircraft is taxying, the flightdeck door opens and the senior member of the cabin staff (known as the Number One) reports that the cabin is secured for take-off and in confirmation she flips over a labelled flap on the centre console which carries a written reminder that this report has been made. This tells the flightdeck crew that all passengers are seated and strapped in, overhead lockers have been checked and closed, and the aisles and access to the main doors are clear. As the aircraft turns at the end of the runway the Captain calls on the cabin PA for cabin staff to take position for take-off. The three stewardesses sit down and secure their seatbelts on foldaway seats, two in the forward entrance

lobby and the other at the after end of the cabin. Once the aircraft had started to taxi, they would have set the main doors to 'automatic' on the Captain's instructions. In this mode, as soon as the doors are opened the

Below:
'...DA101 is cleared for take-off...'. A pilot's-eye view of Runway 25 as he lines up for take-off.

Bottom:
Time for the approach checks, which are called up on the central display. The fuel gauges, at the top of the picture, show 1,500kg remaining in each of the wing tanks.

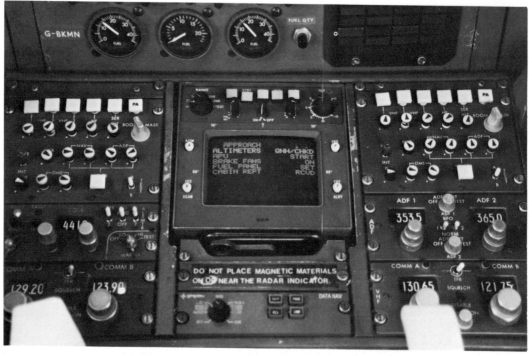

inflatable evacuation chutes will automatically deploy. Being seated by the doors, the cabin crew would be well placed to supervise the evacuation of the aircraft in the event of an incident on take-off or landing.

Reaching the end of the runway, the First Officer slows the aircraft down using the foot brakes and moves over to the left-hand side of the runway to give room to swing round to the right through 180° to line up ready for take-off. As the aircraft straightens up, he checks for full and unrestricted movement of the control column and rudder pedals, and looks for the indication of roll spoiler deployment with movement of the wheel on the column. The anti-collision strobe lights are switched on and also the landing lights if required. A final glance at the MWS panel shows only green captions illuminated and the aircraft is ready to go.

While the turn at the end of the runway is being completed, the Captain calls the Tower:

Captain: 'Dan-Air one zero one is ready for departure.'
Newcastle Tower: 'Dan-Air one zero one is cleared for take-off. Surface wind two seven zero degrees at one three knots.'
Captain: Dan-Air one zero one, cleared for take-off.'

The time is 0612 as the brakes are released and the thrust levers are moved fully forward. With the First Officer flying the aircraft, the Captain starts the stop watch as the 146 begins to roll forward and checks that both ASIs are beginning to read as speed increases. He also checks that the engine instruments are showing correct readings with the N1 indication building and stabilising at the bugged 91%. Initially, Andy steers as he has while taxying, by means of a small tiller on his right-hand side but, as the Captain calls '80 knots', he transfers to full control by the rudder. In quick succession the Captain calls 'V1' and 'VR'. The former indicates that the decision speed has been reached and the take-off must now continue whatever happens, even if an engine fails, and at the second call the First Officer pulls back firmly but gently to rotate the aircraft to a flying attitude and DA101 is airborne.

The speed continues to increase rapidly, and in the next few seconds the Captain calls 'V2' and then, having looked at both Vertical Speed Indicators (VSI), announces 'Positive rate of climb'. This is final and vital confirmation that the aircraft is actually airborne and climbing as it should be. It might be thought that this obvious fact could be verified by looking out of the window, but in conditions of fog or low

The First Officer pulls back the control column firmly but gently to rotate the aircraft to a flying attitude.

cloud, or at night, this is not always possible and the impartial evidence of the instruments is more reliable.

With V2 safely attained, the First Officer calls 'Gear up' and the Captain reaches across, moves the red undercarriage lever to the 'up' position, and monitors the three lights which glow red and then green as the gear travels and locks in the 'up' position. As confirmation, the rumbling aerodynamic noise audible in the cockpit from the extended nosewheel stops and a slight clunk is felt as the wheels lock in the retracted position. Freed of the drag from the undercarriage, the 146 continues to accelerate and the First Officer calls 'Flaps up' as the speed passes 150kt. The Captain moves the flap lever, on the right-hand side of the centre console, forward to the fully up position and the retraction causes a further lessening of aerodynamic noise, not particularly noticeable on the flightdeck, but more so in the passenger cabin.

In accordance with the noise abatement procedure, Andy keeps the aircraft on a heading of 250° until passing 1,000ft on the QFE, before turning left on to a heading of 215° to make good a course for the Ribel intersection, 64 miles away. The 1,000ft point is quickly passed and power is increased for the climb to Flight Level 230. This is attained not by moving the thrust levers, but by selecting maximum continuous thrust on the TMS. This action will cause the engines to operate at a TGT which can be set by means of a knob at the lower edge of the TMS panel, today selected at 840°. With this power set, the aircraft continues to accelerate to a speed of 250kt (IAS) and settles into an initial rate of climb of just over 2,000ft/min. As the 146 banks in the left turn, the tower calls:

Newcastle Tower: 'Dan-Air one zero one airborne at one two. Contact Newcastle Radar one two six decimal three five.'
Captain: 'Dan-Air one zero one to Radar. Good Day.'

Reaching down to the VHF radio controls on the centre console, he switches to Channel B on the VHF2 set where frequency 126.35MHz has already been selected and checks in with Radar.

Below:
The cabin has been reported secure for landing.

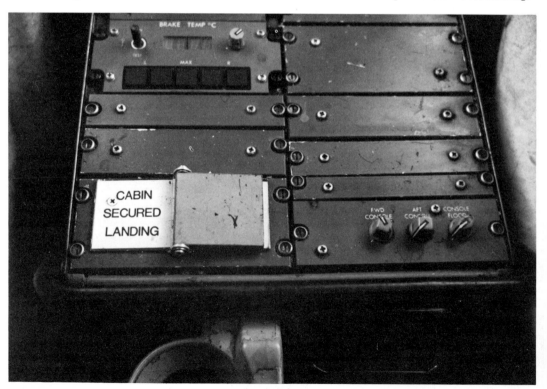

		18°	24°	30°
	31000 kg			
V_R		111	103	97
V_1		124	115	106
V_{2TO}		159	159	159
V_{ER}			166	
$V_{REF\,25}$			109	
		30°	24°	18°	0°
V_{REF}		114	120	130	165

Above:
Shortly after take-off, the engine instruments show full power is being developed. Note the white pointers of the N1 indicators (2nd row down) up against the preset marker bugs. The reference card shows the speeds for the 31,000kg take-off weight.

Left:
Located on the centre console, each pilot has access to the aircraft's communications system. The top panel is the station box which selects the speech and audio channels fed to each pilot's headset. In the centre are the ADF frequency selectors, and below that are the selectors for the VHF radio channels, set up for Newcastle Tower (119.7) and Approach (126.35).

23

Captain: 'Newcastle Radar, Dan-Air one zero one is in the left turn for Ribel, passing two thousand feet.'

Newcastle Radar: 'Roger Dan-Air one zero one. Report passing Flight Level five zero.'

Captain: 'One zero one.'

The aircraft is now settled on a heading of 215° and still maintaining a climb rate of 2,000ft/min. Until now the First Officer has been flying the aircraft manually, but he now reaches across to the left-hand side of the glareshield and presses the Vertical Speed (VS) and Heading (HDG) buttons on the autopilot control panel. The autopilot will now keep the aircraft on the heading of 215° which has been set by rotating the bug on the HSD to the required figure, and any further changes of course can be effected merely by rotating the bug to the new heading. Apart from the final approach at Gatwick, the aircraft will be steered by this method for the rest of the flight.

For climbing or descending, the autopilot offers two modes of operation: with VS selected, the aircraft will maintain the rate of climb or descent effective at the moment of pressing the button. Alternatively, the ALT (altitude) button can be selected when the aircraft will climb or descend at a variable rate depending upon the method of operation, but will level out as soon as a preset altitude or level is reached. For the moment, the cleared level of 230 has been set, but the ALT control has not been selected.

The aircraft is now on track for Ribel, an imaginary point located on a bearing of 215° from the Newcastle VOR at a range of 64 miles on the DME. The required course (or radial) from the VOR can be maintained by dialling up 215 on the course selector associated with the VHF navigation set selected, and engaging the LNAV mode on the autopilot. The aircraft will then continuously adjust its heading to stay on this radial. Alternatively, the bearing from the VOR can be monitored on the appropriate pointer on the HSD and the heading bug adjusted to keep the aircraft on course. After departure from Newcastle, the left turn has established the aircraft just to the west of the correct track; by maintaining a heading of 215°, the westerly winds will gradually cause it to drift on to the desired track where a small adjustment of the heading bug will serve to cancel out the drift.

There are a few more actions to be carried out following the departure. On passing 3,000ft, both pilots set the barometric subscale on their altimeters to read 1013mb, so both

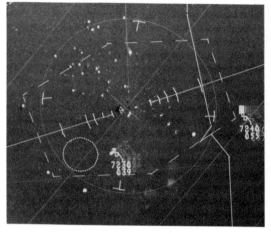

Above:

The radar display at Newcastle shows DA101, identified by the 7230 Squawk given out by the aircraft's Transponder. The height readout shows 3,900ft.

instruments will register Flight Levels rather than altitude above sea level or height above aerodrome; the standby altimeter remains on QNH. The brake cooling fans are switched off, landing lights are checked 'off', and passing 4,000ft the APU is switched off. There has been a little turbulence since take-off caused by the westerly breeze eddying over the hills to the west of Newcastle, but this has now died down and the Captain reaches up and switches off the 'Fasten Seat Belts' and 'No Smoking' signs in the passenger cabin.

The significance of Ribel is that it is the point at which the aircraft will enter controlled airspace and join the airways route system which will take it to Gatwick. Actually, Ribel is on the centreline of Airway Blue 4 and the boundary is five miles east of the centreline. Between Newcastle and Ribel, DA101 is flying in uncontrolled airspace where it could meet military or civil traffic flying at any altitude. Newcastle radar therefore keeps a watch on the aircraft as it climbs, providing a Radar Advisory Service (RAS) under which the controller will issue instructions to alter course, if necessary, in order to maintain at least five miles separation from any unidentified aircraft (unidentified in this context refers to aircraft not being controlled by Newcastle or whose identity and intentions have not been reported to Newcastle by another ATC radar unit). Before DA101 can enter the airways system it must be cleared to do so by the Pole Hill sector of the LATCC at West Drayton near London-Heathrow Airport. Thus, while the aircraft continues its climb, the Approach

Controller at Newcastle contacts the Sector Controller by means of the ATC telephone network and a clearance is issued which will keep the 146 safely separated from the busy morning traffic on the airways. When, as requested, the Captain reports passing Flight Level 50, the Newcastle Radar Controller is ready to come back with the airways joining clearance for the aircraft. Incidentally, the call 'passing five zero' enables the controller to verify the altitude readout shown on the radar from the responses of the aircraft's Transponder.

First Officer: 'Newcastle, Dan-Air one zero one is passing Flight Level five zero.'
Newcastle Radar: 'Roger one zero one. You are cleared to join controlled airspace northeast of Ribel at Flight Level one nine zero or above, climbing to maintain Flight Level two three zero. Request level change en route to Flight Level two seven zero.'

The First Officer acknowledges this clearance and continues to monitor the climb on his instruments. In the passenger cabin the stewardesses are beginning to serve up a hot breakfast but, with a proper sense of priorities, the Number One comes forward to the flightdeck with two very welcome cups of coffee. For the moment all is going smoothly and the crew can relax for a couple of minutes. It is a fine morning and on the starboard side there is a good view of the Pennine Hills, while out to port can be seen the east coast stretching down to the Humber Estuary, easily picked out because of the sunlight reflecting off the water.

With the autopilot locked in the VS mode, the airspeed begins to drop as the aircraft seeks to maintain the rate of climb, and so IAS mode is selected instead. This maintains the speed of around 250kt and allows the rate of climb to decay with increasing altitude, although even at the higher levels 1,500ft/min is still being achieved.

At 0618 there is another call from Newcastle:

Newcastle Radar: 'Dan-Air one zero one, Squawk four four one zero.'

The Captain acknowledges this call and sets the new code on the transponder. There is a short pause while the Controller checks that the change of code appears on his screen, then he transfers control of the aircraft to the Pole Hill Sector at LATCC.

Newcastle Radar: 'Dan-Air one zero one, your position is three six miles bearing two one five from Newcastle. There is a DC-9 airborne out of Tees-side also climbing towards Ribel. Contact London Control on one three one decimal zero five.'
Captain: 'London on one three one decimal zero five, Dan-Air one zero one. Good day Newcastle.'

Both pilots reach down and select 131.05 on their VHF boxes and the Captain selects the appropriate channel.

Captain: 'London Control this is Dan-Air one zero one. We are passing Flight Level one six zero and cleared to two three zero. Squawking four four one zero.'
London Control: 'Dan-Air one zero one Squawk ident. Maintain two three zero. WILLO One arrival at Gatwick, Runway two six.'

The Captain acknowledges this call and presses the 'Ident' button on the transponder. Although the controller for the Pole Hill sector is actually at West Drayton, his radar screen shows a composite picture made up of information from many radars sited around the country. Thus he can see DA101 approaching Ribel displaying the 4410 code which he has already allocated. When the pilot presses the 'Ident' button the transponder sends out a double response which is picked up by the ground radar's data processing system, where the code is matched with the Flight Plan information already stored in its memory. The 4410 on the radar screen is then replaced with DA101, the aircraft's callsign. With this procedure complete, the controller checks the other traffic on the airway and speaks again to the aircraft.

London Control: 'Dan-Air one zero one, continue climb to Flight Level two seven zero.'

Again, the Captain acknowledges and resets the autopilot altitude control to 27,000ft. Shortly afterwards, the DC-9 from Tees-side is heard calling London and it is apparent that it is well below and behind, so the controller does not need to restrict the second aircraft to achieve the necessary separation. Shortly after this the 146 runs into a layer of alto stratus cloud at 19,000ft, but at 21,000ft the aircraft is in brilliant sunshine and on top of all cloud layers. At this point a routine scan of the engine instruments shows 91.5% N1, 92% N2 and the TGTs averaging 820°C. Fuel flow is

700kg/hr for each engine and total consumption since start-up is 680kg.

The First Officer now consults with the Captain and selects the Honiley VOR on NAV1, leaving the Barton VOR still on NAV2. As the aircraft passes over Ribel, he leans forward and makes a slight adjustment to the heading bug in order to keep on course for Barton. However, no sooner are these actions completed than a call from ATC leads to a change of course:

London Control: 'Dan-Air one zero one is now cleared direct to Honiley.'

This call is made at 0626, just as the aircraft is about to level at Flight Level 270, so the Captain is able to report this when he acknowledges the instruction.

Captain: 'Dan-Air one zero one direct to Honiley. Now level at two seven zero.'

During the last few minutes of the climb, the First Officer has selected 128.6 on his VHF box in order to listen to the London VOLMET broadcast. This continuously transmits the half-hourly weather reports for the major UK airfields, including Heathrow and Gatwick. The weather observations are made at each airport at 10min to and 20min past each hour, and the reports are available on the VOLMET about 10 minutes later. Currently the Captain jots down the 0550 Gatwick weather which gives the surface wind as 340° at 5kt, visibility in excess of 10km, a small amount of cloud at 3,500ft, temperature 10°C, dew point 7°C and the QNH is 1022mb. The Heathrow and Bournemouth weathers are similar, so there is no problem in the unlikely event of a diversion from Gatwick becoming necessary. In the winter, the crew would be closely watching the temperature and dew point on the weather reports as this gives an indication of the likelihood of fog forming, but there are no such worries today.

Levelling off at Flight Level 270, the First Officer checks the performance tables to ascertain the optimum cruising Mach number, given the aircraft's weight and altitude. This works out at Mach 0.68 and he adjusts the thrust levers to achieve this speed before synchronising on No 2 engine by means of the

TMS. With the aircraft on course for Honiley, he selects the Midhurst VOR on NAV 1 as this will be the next point to head for after passing Honiley. Presently, a heading of 174° is set on the HSD bug to keep the aircraft on course, and the DME shows a readout of 84 miles to run to Honiley which is just south of Birmingham.

For the moment there is little for the crew to do as far as flying the aircraft is concerned, so a few of the routine tasks can be carried out. The First Officer speaks to the passengers and tells them that the aircraft is passing over Manchester with Liverpool in sight on the right-hand side. He gives them a brief description of the weather at Gatwick (fine but cool) and confirms that the flight is due to land on schedule. As they listen to this information, the passengers are tucking into a tasty hot breakfast which is a standard feature of Dan-Air's early-morning scheduled flights. This is a facility much appreciated by the business traveller who has had to make a very early start in order to catch the flight, and has probably missed a proper meal at home before leaving for the airport.

Next, the First Officer checks the fuel remaining, reading the figures from the three tank gauges set below the engine instruments; he calculates the remaining flying time available by plotting the figure on a simple graph printed on the flight log. A diagonal line already drawn on this graph shows 'hours to go' against 'fuel remaining'. As long as fuel consumption on the flight is more or less as expected, then the plotted fuel reading will be above or on the line. If it is below, then the aircraft does not have sufficient fuel to complete its flight with the required reserves and a diversion may become necessary. However, this rarely happens and is usually due to adverse winds being considerably stronger than forecast. Today all is well and the First Officer is able to confirm that the landing weight of the aircraft will be as calculated before departure. He therefore takes the information flip card from its clip on his panel and turns it over to display the relevant speeds for a weight of 29,000kg, the closest approximation to the calculated landing weight of 29,443kg. The cards are then replaced on the clip.

The First Officer now turns his attention to preparing the charts for landing at Gatwick. On initial contact with London a 'WILLO One' arrival was specified and this is known as a standard arrival route (STAR) procedure. Such procedures simplify air traffic control's task in dealing with complex traffic situations in the busy London Terminal Control Area (TMA)

H1	⌐H
12 FEB 87	

Trans alt 6000 | **Trans lev ATC**

1. Cross Speed Limit Points at Max IAS 250kt, & HOLLY at Max IAS 220kt.
2. If D/A D129 active route HON-WCO-WOD-MID.
3. When DO35 is inactive & a/c routed ORTAC/KATHY-R1, join WLO 1C at SELSI.
4. WILLO hold (Max IAS 220kt). If over subscribed use 'GWC' hold.
5. If MID VOR/DME u/s use ASTRA STARs. If MID becomes u/s in WILLO hold transfer to ASTRA hold.

NOT TO SCALE

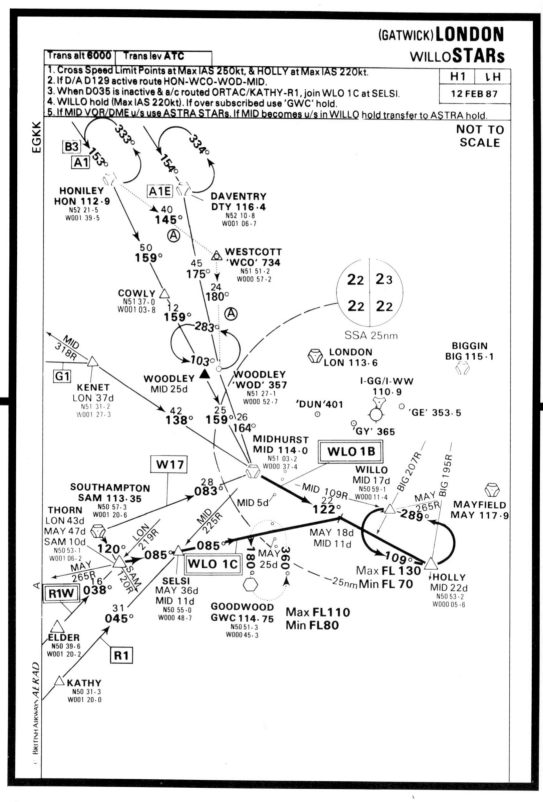

EGKK

© BRITISH AIRWAYS, ALRAD

28

which encompasses the airspace surrounding Heathrow and Gatwick airports. Under a STAR, aircraft fly set routeings at specified speeds in order to reach a point from where they can be directed to final approach by radar, or alternatively be instructed to take up a holding pattern while awaiting their turn to join the landing sequence. 'WILLO' takes its name from a point defined by the intersection of VOR radials, or bearings, and is some 10 miles south of Gatwick Airport.

Also required is the chart showing the ILS procedure for landing on Runway 26 Left, and finally the ground chart showing taxying routes and parking bays for use after landing. All these charts are taken from the *Aerad Flight Guide* and are inserted in clear plastic envelopes which are clipped to the side of the cockpit where they are easily visible to both pilots. As this is completed there is a call from ATC:

Left:
An Arrival Chart for Gatwick, showing the WILLO STAR. The aircraft's route will be from Honiley, via Midhurst, to HOLLY. The airport is shown by the circular symbol below the letters I-GG. *AERAD Chart*

Above:
The time is 0639 and DA101 is descending through Flight Level 230. The DME readouts above the HSD show that Honiley is now 5.3 miles astern and the Midhurst VOR 83.9 miles ahead.

London Control: 'Dan-Air one zero one, report your heading.'
Captain: 'Heading one seven four, Dan-Air one zero one.'
London Control: 'Dan-Air one zero one turn right heading one eight five.'

The First Officer leans forward to turn the heading bug on the HSD to the new figure. The 146 banks gently to the right and quickly settles on the new course. The DME readout shows the aircraft to be 50 miles north of Honiley and it is being steered by ATC towards the western side of the Airway Upper Amber One in order to keep clear of northbound traffic from the London TMA, and other traffic heading south climbing out of Manchester.

As soon as the aircraft is steady on its new heading, ATC calls again:

London Control: 'Dan-Air one zero one contact London Control on one two nine

decimal two and report your heading.'
Captain: 'Dan-Air one zero one to one two nine decimal two.'

The time is 0632 as both pilots select VHF1 which is switched to the new frequency and the Captain makes the initial call:

Captain: 'London Control, Dan-Air one zero one is on frequency heading one eight five degrees. Requesting descent in three minutes.'

The flight has now come under the control of the Daventry Sector at LATCC — this Controller will be responsible for looking after the aircraft as it begins its descent towards the London TMA alongside the rest of the traffic stream which is building up as aircraft from several UK airports converge on the capital. The crew are looking to leave Flight Level 270 at a point 20 miles north of Honiley, which is now 45 miles to the south, but the exact point will depend on clearance from ATC. A couple of minutes later this clearance is forthcoming:

London Control 'Dan-Air one zero one descend to Flight Level one three zero, to be level four zero miles before Midhurst.'

The Midhurst VOR is some 87 miles south of Honiley and its frequency (114.0MHz) has previously been selected on NAV1 with Honiley switched to NAV2. It should be noted that at this point in the flight the aircraft is steering headings as directed by ATC and therefore the readings from the navigation aids are for information only. As the DME readout shows 20 miles to run to Honiley, the First Officer throttles back to approximately 68% N1 and allows the aircraft's nose to drop with the reduced power. With a rate of descent of 1,500ft/min established, he selects VS mode on the autopilot to hold this rate. The change of level is reported to ATC by the Captain:

Captain: 'Dan-Air one zero one is leaving Flight Level two seven zero.'

This call is acknowledged and the First Officer then selects 130.65MHz, the Dan-Air company frequency, and calls Operations at Gatwick using the aircraft's registration rather than the trip number as a callsign:

First Officer: 'Dan Ops, this is Mike November inbound to Gatwick as the one zero one with fifty-eight passengers. We should be on chocks at ten minutes past the hour and the aircraft is serviceable.'

Operations acknowledge this call and record the information so that the necessary arrangements can be put in train to receive the flight. If, for example, there were any significant unserviceabilities an Engineer could be instructed to meet the aircraft so that repairs could be effected; any passengers requiring special handling could also be provided for. After this exchange, the First Officer reselects VHF1 to monitor the ATC frequency. Shortly afterwards another heading change is passed:

London Control: 'Dan-Air one zero one turn left, heading one five five.'

Again, an adjustment to the heading bug brings the aircraft on to course and, with the descent established, some of the descent checks are carried out. The Captain reaches up to the overhead panel and sets up the cabin pressurisation system by adjusting the dial so that the Gatwick airfield altitude is shown. The system will then automatically adjust the cabin conditions as the aircraft descends, although in this mode the rate of change can sometimes be a bit fierce and crews will often use a manual override to give a greater degree of control and ensure passenger comfort.

As the aircraft will be manoeuvring during the approach phase of the flight, the 'Fasten Seat Belt' signs are switched on to ensure that the passengers are safely strapped in. This also serves as a warning to the cabin crew that they should now be in the process of clearing away the meal trays and preparing the cabin for landing. As if on cue, one of the stewardesses looks in on the flightdeck to clear away the crew's coffee cups and the Captain takes the opportunity to advise her that they should be landing in about 20min.

The descent continues and the First Officer checks over the approach charts, then carries out a briefing on the landing procedure, together with actions in the event of a 'Go Around'. The landing data is checked and confirmed, and the necessary figures are set on ASI and TMS bugs. These checks cover the landing distance required which is affected by the aircraft's weight, the air temperature and the surface windspeed and direction. Given the length of Gatwick's runway, there are not usually any problems, but a strong crosswind might force a diversion.

V ref, the target speed at the runway threshold, is set on the ASI bug and, in preparation for a possible 'Go Around', the appropriate N1 setting is bugged on the engine gauges. In the event of an overshoot being initiated, the throttles can be pushed fully forward to give maximum available power automatically, leaving the crew free to fly the aircraft.

Next is a final check on the weather landing minima and, although this should be no problem today, the 'Decision Heights' are bugged on the altimeters. This is the height at which a 'Go Around' would be initiated if neither pilot had visual contact with the runway on final approach.

When the 146 passes Honiley at 0639, the First Officer selects frequency 117.9MHz on NAV2 which tunes him into the Mayfield VOR situated southeast of Gatwick. At this stage he does not need it for navigation purposes, but he can listen in to the Automatic Terminal Information Service (ATIS) which gives out a continuous transmission of the current Gatwick weather and runway conditions, together with the runway in use and the altimeter pressure settings (QNH and QFE). Each time the information is updated it is given a reference code — in this case 'Golf'. The First Officer copies the information while the Captain deals with another call from ATC:

London Control: 'Dan-Air one zero one is cleared direct to Midhurst.'

The call is acknowledged and the First Officer checks his HSD to see that the VOR is bearing 159° with 65 miles to run. He adjusts his heading bug to maintain that track and, for the time being, responsibility for navigation of the aircraft reverts to the crew. A few minutes later, as the 146 passes over Oxford clearly visible below as the morning haze disperses, ATC instruct the crew to change frequency to 132.05MHz. This call is acknowledged and the Captain calls on the new frequency:

Captain: 'Dan-Air one zero one is passing Flight Level one five zero for one three zero.'
London Control: 'Roger one zero one. Maintain one three zero. No delay at Gatwick.'

The aircraft is now being controlled by the TMA South Sector at LATCC who will be responsible for steering it through the western edge of the London TMA above the outbound traffic from Heathrow and Gatwick and position it, with other Gatwick inbounds, to a point where Gatwick Radar can take control for the final stages. In a short time the aircraft is given further descent clearance:

London Control: 'Dan-Air one zero one descend to Flight Level one zero zero.'

The Captain acknowledges and continues the descent on course for Midhurst. Above the cloud and haze layer it is exceptionally clear and several other aircraft are visible. Over on the left can be seen a couple of aircraft holding over the Bovingdon VOR awaiting their turn in the landing sequence at Heathrow; a few miles ahead and below is a British Airtours TriStar also inbound to Gatwick. At this point the No 1 stewardess comes forward to report that the cabin is secured for landing and turns over the telltale flap on the centre console in confirmation. The Captain advises her that they will be landing in about 10 minutes, all being well.

At 06.51 the aircraft is approaching Flight Level 100; the First Officer engages the Altitude Lock on the autopilot which automatically cuts out the VS mode. As the aircraft has been descending, each successive level that it is cleared to by ATC is set on the autopilot altitude selector panel, and so by selecting the ALT mode the aircraft levels off automatically at Flight Level 100. He adjusts the power settings to maintain a speed of 250kt and prepares to turn left on to a heading of 122° as Midhurst is passed in order to conform with the WILLO STAR.

Midhurst is crossed at 0652 and, as the heading bug is wound round to the new heading, ATC comes up with the next frequency change:

London Control: 'Dan-Air one zero one contact Gatwick Approach on one one nine decimal six.'

The new frequency is dialled up on VHF1 while, at the same time, 110.9MHz is selected on NAV2 in order to tune into the ILS for landing on Runway 26 Left at Gatwick. The Captain calls Gatwick as directed while the First Officer is setting up the ILS.

Below:
At Flight Level 100 (approximately 10,000ft) over Midhurst, the visibility is almost unlimited in the bright morning sun but a broken cloud layer can be seen to the southeast over the Gatwick area.

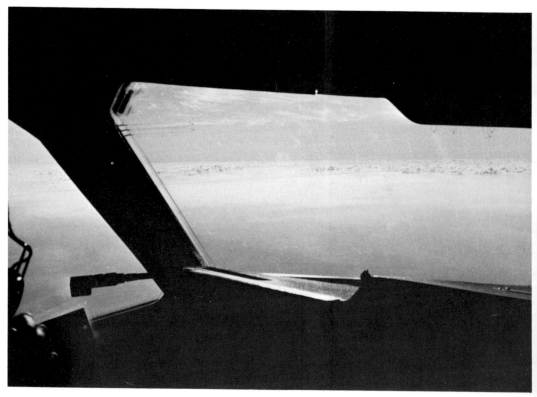

Captain: 'Gatwick Approach, Dan-Air one zero one is a one four six with information golf.'
Gatwick Approach: 'Roger Dan-Air one zero one, cleared to HOLLY for WILLO Arrival. What is your speed?'
Captain: 'Two five zero knots, one zero one.'

Five miles past Midhurst is a Speed Limit Point, beyond which aircraft are obliged to fly at speeds of 250kt or less. ATC may require a particular speed to be maintained in order to achieve a suitable position in the traffic sequence, hence the query as to DA101's actual speed at that point. Holly is a point 22 miles bearing 122° from Midhurst and the aircraft will take up a racetrack holding pattern on reaching there unless otherwise instructed by ATC.

A couple of minutes after passing Midhurst, further instructions are indeed forthcoming:

Gatwick Approach: 'Dan-Air one zero one turn left heading one zero zero.'

This instruction, acknowledged and acted upon by the First Officer, is significant because it implies that the Gatwick Radar controller has now taken control of the aircraft which is no longer bound by the procedures laid down in the STAR. From now on ATC will issue the necessary instructions to direct the 146 on to final approach for Runway 26, where it will lock on to the ILS for landing. A few seconds later there is a further instruction:

Gatwick Approach: 'Dan-Air one zero one descend to four thousand feet on QNH one zero two two.'
Captain: 'One zero one descending to four thousand on one zero two two. Leaving one zero zero.'

4,000ft is dialled up on the Autopilot Altitude Selector by the Captain while the First Officer throttles back slightly to allow the aircraft to start descending. It stabilises in the descent with the engine gauges showing N1 at 64%, TGT around 420 and fuel flow right back to 150kg/hr.

On leaving Flight Level 100 it is time to carry out the approach checks and these are now run through as the aircraft descends. Both pilots' altimeters have the QNH of 1,022mb set on their subscales and the Captain, as monitoring pilot, calls out 'One zero two two set, reading eight thousand four hundred.' The First Officer sets his own and checks that it is reading the figure called out by the Captain.

Several items now prepare the aircraft for landing. The APU is started and is monitored as it spools up to 100% rpm, the EGT not exceeding 870°C as it does so. A green annunciator light should show when electrical power is available, normally 4sec after reaching 95% rpm. The wheel-brake fans are switched on and again a green light should indicate satisfactory operation. The fuel control panel is checked and all pumps are selected 'on'. Finally, a check that the cabin is secure, already reported by the stewardess and shown by the telltale flap. The instructions from ATC are now coming at an increased rate:

Gatwick Approach: 'Dan-Air one zero one, turn left heading zero eight zero, downwind leg for runway two six left, number four'.
Captain: 'One zero one.'

The aircraft is now about seven miles south of Gatwick and flying parallel to the runway prior to turning in for final approach. The controller has advised the crew that DA101 is fourth in line to land and there must, therefore, be three aircraft ahead. One of these is the British Airtours TriStar which was seen earlier, but the aircraft immediately ahead is a British Caledonian DC-10, callsign BeeCal two five four.

With the 146 now under radar direction, there is no need to use the VORs for navigation and the Captain selects the ILS on NAV1 so that both sets are tuned to it for landing. As the aircraft runs downwind, the ILS receiver will not yet pick up the Localiser signal which defines the final approach track lined up with the runway, and so a red flag shows on the ADI warning the pilots to ignore the ILS indications for the moment.

Ahead can be heard the British Caledonian DC-10 (BR254) reporting through Flight Level 80 in his descent, whereupon he is instructed to change frequency to Gatwick Director. The same instruction is passed to this aircraft:

Gatwick Approach: 'Dan-Air one zero one, contact Gatwick Director on one one eight decimal six.'

With the frequency change made, the Captain calls up:

Captain: 'Gatwick Director, Dan-Air one zero one'.
Gatwick Director: 'Dan-Air one zero one, descend to three thousand feet QNH and reduce speed to two one zero knots.'

33

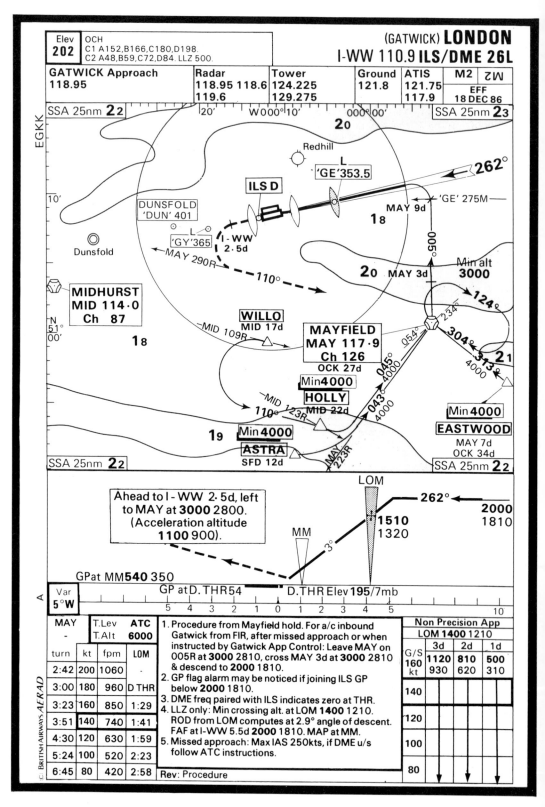

Elev **202** | OCH C1 A152,B166,C180,D198. C2 A48,B59,C72,D84. LLZ 500.

(GATWICK) **LONDON**
I-WW 110.9 **ILS/DME 26L**

| GATWICK Approach 118.95 | Radar 118.95 118.6 119.6 | Tower 124.225 129.275 | Ground 121.8 | ATIS 121.75 117.9 | M2 ZW EFF 18 DEC 86 |

EGKK

SSA 25nm **22** 20' W000°10' 000°00' SSA 25nm **23**
20

Redhill
L 'GE' 353.5
ILS D 262°
DUNSFOLD 'DUN' 401 'GE' 275M
L 'GY' 365 MAY 9d
I-WW 2·5d 18
MAY 290R 005°
Dunsfold 110° 20 MAY 3d Min alt 3000
124°
MIDHURST MID 114·0 Ch 87 MID 109R 234°
18 WILLO MID 17d MAYFIELD MAY 117·9 Ch 126 OCK 27d 045° 4000 304° 313° 21 4000
054°
MID 123R Min **4000** 043° 4000
110° HOLLY MID 22d 043° 4000 Min **4000**
19 Min **4000** EASTWOOD MAY 7d OCK 34d
ASTRA SFD 12d MAY 223R
SSA 25nm **22** SSA 25nm **22**

LOM
Ahead to I-WW 2·5d, left to MAY at **3000** 2800. (Acceleration altitude **1100** 900). 262° 2000 1810
MM **1510** 1320
3°
GP at MM **540** 350
GP at D. THR 54 D. THR Elev **195**/7mb

A
Var **5°W** 5 4 3 2 1 0 1 2 3 4 5 10

MAY –	T.Lev **ATC** T.Alt **6000**		
turn	kt	fpm	LOM
2:42	200	1060	-
3:00	180	960	D THR
3:23	160	850	1:29
3:51	140	740	1:41
4:30	120	630	1:59
5:24	100	520	2:23
6:45	80	420	2:58

1. Procedure from Mayfield hold. For a/c inbound Gatwick from FIR, after missed approach or when instructed by Gatwick App Control: Leave MAY on 005R at **3000** 2810, cross MAY 3d at **3000** 2810 & descend to **2000** 1810.
2. GP flag alarm may be noticed if joining ILS GP below **2000** 1810.
3. DME freq paired with ILS indicates zero at THR.
4. LLZ only: Min crossing alt. at LOM **1400** 1210. ROD from LOM computes at 2.9° angle of descent. FAF at I-WW 5.5d **2000** 1810. MAP at MM.
5. Missed approach: Max IAS 250kts, if DME u/s follow ATC instructions.

Rev: Procedure

Non Precision App			
LOM **1400** 1210			
G/S	3d	2d	1d
160 kt	**1120** 930	810 620	500 310
140			
120			
100			
80			

C: BRITISH AIRWAYS AERAD

34

Andy, the First Officer, reduces the power settings while maintaining a steady 1,500ft-/min descent rate, although it will be difficult to achieve 210kt until the aircraft is levelled off at 3,000ft. In the meantime, the new cleared altitude is set on the Autopilot Selector with the aircraft still being flown in the ALT and HDG modes.

By this time the aircraft is passing 4,500ft and is just running into the top of a broken cloud layer. The QFE of 1015mb is set on the First Officer's altimeter to give a height above the runway reference for landing. On that setting 2,800ft will be equivalent to 3,000ft on the QNH as the airfield elevation is 202ft.

Gatwick Director: 'Dan-Air one zero one turn left heading three six zero degrees.'

Acknowledging the instruction, Andy turns the heading bug on the HSI to bring the 146 on to a northerly heading. On this track it is routeing at 90° to the final approach track and is beginning to come into the ILS Localiser beam which radiates for 35° on either side of the approach centreline. Consequently, after a few hesitant movements, the Localiser flag disappears on the ADI shortly followed by the Glidepath flag.

The Instrument Landing System (ILS) is a ground-based navigation aid which was perfected shortly after World War 2 and is currently the standard approach aid at all the world's main airports. It consists of two transmitters, the Localiser and Glidepath, which respectively send out radio beams defining the approach centreline to the runway and a 3° vertical angle of approach. An associated DME installation gives the pilot a readout of distance to run to touchdown. Most modern aircraft, including the BAe146, are equipped to process the signals from the ILS to the autopilot so that the aircraft will automatically 'lock on' to the Localiser and Glidepath and fly the correct approach profile unaided until the decision height is reached. At this point the pilot will disengage the autopilot and land the aircraft normally unless it is equipped with some form of Autoland equipment.

As DA101 reaches 3,000ft heading north, the autopilot levels it off and speed rapidly reduces to the stipulated 210kt. The First Officer increases the power settings to maintain that speed resulting in a N1 reading of 80%, TGT of 545°C and fuel flow at 450kg/hr (per engine). Peter reports the level:

Captain: 'Dan-Air one zero one is level at three thousand feet.'
Gatwick Director: 'Roger one zero one, you are one seven miles from touchdown. Number three.'

So there is just the TriStar and the DC-10 ahead; the former has just reported established on the ILS and is told to contact Gatwick Tower. The BR254 also reports level at 3,000ft although he is not visible due to the patches of cloud.

Gatwick Director: 'Dan-Air one zero one reduce speed to one eight zero knots.'
Captain: 'One zero one reducing.'

A slight reduction in the power settings, and the airspeed begins to decay as instructed. At this moment there is a sudden jolt as the aircraft hits a patch of turbulence, almost certainly caused by the wake vortex of the DC-10 ahead. The Captain reports this to the controller, concerned that the DC-10 may be too close.

Captain: 'Gatwick, Dan-Air one zero one, we have just run through the slipstream of the DC-10.'
Gatwick Director: 'Roger one zero one, the DC-10 is eight miles ahead of you. Turn left heading two nine zero to report established.'

Eight miles is the minimum separation which ATC are obliged to provide between the DC-10 and the BAe146 due to the turbulence created by the wide-bodied aircraft, and it is easy to see from this why a lesser separation is not permitted. The instruction to report 'established' means that the aircraft is free to turn on to the final approach track when the ILS signals indicate that it is intercepting the centreline. On a heading of 290° it is closing the centreline at an angle of 30° which will allow the autopilot to execute a relatively gentle turn to lock on to the Localiser.

In order to allow the autopilot to acquire and follow the ILS signals, the Captain selects the GSL mode (Glideslope and Localiser) on the push-button control panel. The DME shows just over 12 miles to run to touchdown and both pilots monitor the ADI and HSD to follow the turn on to the Localiser. On the HSD, the Localiser beam is represented by an orange bar which moves left or right according to the aircraft's relative displacement from the centreline. At first glance this appears to work in the wrong sense in that if the aircraft is offset to the left then the bar floats to the right. However, the instrument acts in the command sense and indicates that the aircraft needs to fly to the right in order to regain the centreline. The angle of closure is shown by the angle of the bar to the vertical which, in turn, indicates the aircraft's heading. A broken orange bar indicates the axis of the ILS centreline and its alignment relative to the aircraft's heading. For an aircraft correctly established on the centreline, the broken bar will be vertically aligned and the smaller offset bar will have centred so that the two now form one continuous bar. In windless conditions the aircraft's heading shown by the outer compass rose will coincide with the alignment of the runway and Localiser.

As DA101 closes the centreline from the left, the autopilot initiates the final turn and the HSD bar floats into the centre showing that the 146 is now established on the centreline. At the same time the Localiser indicator on the ADI, which consists of a simple vertical white bar, also settles in the centre of the instrument. The Captain reports the fact to ATC:

Captain: 'Dan-Air one zero one is established.'
Gatwick Director: 'Roger one zero one, you are one one miles from touchdown. Contact Tower one two four decimal two two.'

Another quick frequency change.

Captain: 'Gatwick Tower, Dan-Air one zero one established at one one miles.'
Gatwick Tower: 'One zero one continue approach. Report at the marker.'

The marker referred to is another component of the ILS and is a fixed radio beacon situated at four miles from touchdown, and gives an aural tone as the aircraft crosses it. At this point the aircraft is below the Glidepath beam which angles up at 3° from the runway, but as the range from touchdown decreases it will intercept the Glideslope and start descending under the control of the autopilot. A small pointer on the right of the HSD indicates the relative position of the aircraft to the Glideslope and works in a similar sense to the Localiser indications in that if the pointer moves up then the aircraft is too low, and vice versa. A horizontal white bar on the ADI performs a similar function.

Just inside 10 miles from touchdown the Glidepath pointers begin to centre and the aircraft starts to descend at approximately 1,000ft/min. Left to its own devices the aircraft speed would increase, so Andy calls for the first stage of flap (18°) and the Captain reaches across to comply. At seven miles from touchdown Andy calls 'undercarriage down', and again the Captain operates the lever, watches the lights change through red to green and confirms 'wheels down and locked'.

The combination of the lowered wheels and flaps causes the airspeed to begin to reduce as the power settings are not altered at this stage. A few final checks are carried out, 'brake pressure OK, APU is "on", engine bleed air "off" '.

Right:
The HSD is the prime navigation display on the aircraft. The outer ring is a compass rose with the aircraft's heading at the top, while the various pointers show the relative bearing of preselected radio beacons. The almost vertical pointer can be slaved to a VOR or ILS Localiser, and the centre segment (here offset to the left) would show displacement from the required line of flight. At the top corners are the DME range readouts and the striped segment on the right would normally show the aircraft's displacement from the Glideslope during an ILS approach.

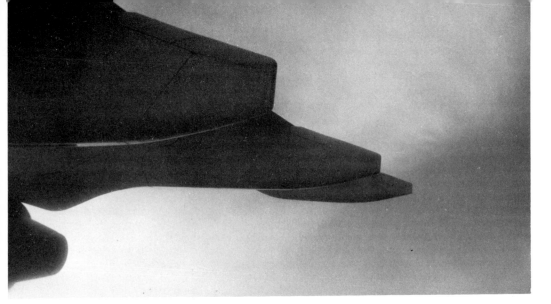

Above:
The flaps are lowered in stages (18, 24, 30 and 33°) for landing. The two inner guide tracks are housed in extensions of the engine pylons and an outer fairing contains the third.

Left:
'. . . flaps 24° . . .'.

Below:
'Full flap, 33°'.

Approaching five miles from touchdown the aircraft passes through 1,500ft and the airspeed is now 165kt. Andy calls 'flaps twenty-four' and the Captain lowers the next stage of flap which further decreases the speed. Ahead, on the runway, is the Caledonian DC-10 as the 146 approaches the marker.

Gatwick Tower: 'BeeCal two five four landed at zero five. Take the next turning right.'

This call is acknowledged and the controller then instructs another aircraft to line up on the runway for take-off. Peter calls, passing the marker:

Captain: 'Dan-Air one zero one passing the marker.'
Gatwick Tower: 'One zero one continue approach. One departure ahead of you.'

At three miles the aircraft is nicely established on both Localiser and Glideslope and both pilots have the runway clearly in sight. They have in fact been able to see the airfield since the aircraft turned on to final approach, but at this point the First Officer disconnects the autopilot and will fly the rest of the approach, and carry out the landing manually. He calls for more flap and the Captain operates the lever to give the 30° setting. This further reduces the airspeed which decays to 140kt at two miles as the aircraft passes 600ft. Approaching one mile, the departing aircraft can be seen lifting off and the Tower calls:

Gatwick Tower: 'Dan-Air one zero one cleared to land. Wind three three zero at eight knots.'
First Officer: 'One zero one is cleared to land.'

Another call brings in the last stage of flaps (33°) as the First Officer concentrates on the final stages of the approach. His target speed at the threshold of the runway is 105kt and, although he has full flap and undercarriage down, the speed has only fallen to 128kt at this stage. However, the BAe146 is fitted with a powerful clamshell door-type airbrake at the rear of the fuselage below the tail. This can be set to any position from fully open to fully closed by means of a lever on the left-hand side of the centre console. Operation of the airbrake causes little or no change of trim and it is an extremely effective method of controlling the airspeed during the final stages of the approach.

Andy now deploys the airbrake to reduce speed to his target 105kt which is achieved as he crosses the end of the runway. Passing through 100ft he pulls the power levers all the way back and the engine note dies to a barely audible whisper. A gentle rearward pressure on the control column brings the aircraft into a slight nose-up attitude at the flare, and as the speed falls off the 146 settles gently on to the runway.

The undercarriage of the 146 is well able to soak up the impacts of even quite hard landings, with the result that the sudden jar which sometimes accompanies an awkward landing in many other airliners is very rarely felt. It is one of the pleasant characteristics of this aircraft which is remarked upon by both crew and passengers. In this case, of course, the smooth landing today is due solely to the skill of the crew!

As soon as the mainwheels touch the runway the First Officer calls for 'spoilers', and the Captain moves the airbrake lever fully back which causes the lift spoilers on the top of the wings to be deployed. This increases the aerodynamic braking and destroys a large proportion of the lift from the wings, anchoring the aircraft firmly to the ground.

Unusually for a civil airliner, the 146 has no reverse thrust and instead relies upon carbon fibre brakes which are extremely effective. However, on a long runway such as Gatwick only gentle braking is necessary using the toe pedals above the rudder bar.

Gatwick Tower: 'Dan-Air one zero one landed at zero seven. Take the next right. Contact Ground on one two one decimal eight.'

The Captain acknowledges the instruction and selects the new frequency.

Captain: 'Gatwick Ground, Dan-Air one zero one vacating the runway.'
Gatwick Ground: 'One zero one taxi on zero eight left for Stand six.'

Gatwick Airport nominally has only one runway and for years has been beset by problems if the runway should become blocked or in need of repair. To cater for this contingency a taxiway running parallel to the runway has been widened and strengthened so that it can be used as an emergency runway. This is known as 08 Left/26 Right as opposed to the main runway which is designated 08 Right/26 Left. The instructions from ground control indicate that DA101 is to use the emergency runway as a taxiway to the main

Left:

Approaching the threshold, another BAe146 is waiting for take-off, together with a British Airtours TriStar. The parallel taxiway, which doubles as an emergency runway, is off to the right.

Below:

. . . as the speed falls off, the BAe146 settles gently on to the runway.

Bottom:

Touchdown!

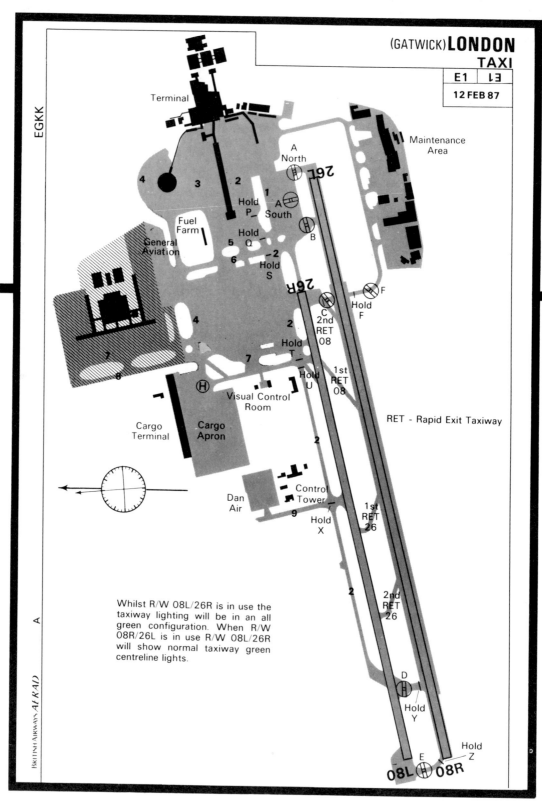

(GATWICK) **LONDON**
TAXI

E1	E1
12 FEB 87	

EGKK

Terminal

Maintenance Area

A North

26L

Hold P
A South
1
2
3
4

B

Fuel Farm

General Aviation

Hold Q
5
6
-2
Hold S

26R

C
2nd RET 08

F
Hold F

7
8

4

2
Hold T

7
Hold U

1st RET 08

RET - Rapid Exit Taxiway

H

Visual Control Room

Cargo Terminal

Cargo Apron

2

Dan Air

Control Tower

9
Hold X

1st RET 26

2

2nd RET 26

Whilst R/W 08L/26R is in use the taxiway lighting will be in an all green configuration. When R/W 08R/26L is in use R/W 08L/26R will show normal taxiway green centreline lights.

D
Hold Y

Hold Z

E
08L 08R

BRITISH AIRWAYS AERAD

A

Above:
The Captain looks out at a Calair DC-10, waiting for it to move clear of the entrance to the parking bay.

Left:
Chart showing Gatwick Airport layout. *AERAD*

Right:
A Ground Engineer marshals DA101 on to its parking spot by Gate 6A.

parking area. Stand 6 is situated on the northern side of the domestic pier and is the one normally used by this particular flight, so the crew are familiar with its position and do not need to consult the airfield chart.

Turning off at the taxiway intersection halfway down the runway, the First Officer runs through the after-landing checks. The airbrakes and spoilers are retracted, as are the wing flaps; correct functioning is indicated by lights and the flap gauge. The brakes are switched to the yellow system and checked by a slight pressure on the pedals. The radar is checked as 'off' (it has not been used on this particular flight), Transponder set to 'standby'. Strobe and landing lights are checked 'off' and a check is made that engine anti-icing systems are off.

It takes a couple of minutes to taxi towards the terminal area and during this time the cabin staff are making a routine announcement to the passengers, informing them of terminal and transport facilities at Gatwick, thanking them for flying with Dan-Air, and adding a final warning that smoking is not permitted until they have entered the terminal building. Approaching the domestic pier, the entrance to the bay containing Stand 6 is occupied by a Calair DC-10 which has pushed back and is starting. The ground controller directs the 146 to wait until the other aircraft has taxied clear so there is a couple of minutes delay before proceeding.

With the DC-10 gone, Andy moves the aircraft forward towards the parking stand, passing a row of recent transatlantic arrivals on the left before swinging hard right into the stand area. Although there are guidelines painted on the tarmac, there is a marshaller available to assist with positioning the aircraft on the correct spot. The 146 moves slowly forward until the stop signal is given and comes to a halt just a few yards away from the pier building.

With the APU already running, its generator is brought on line and the engine-powered generators deselected. The parking brake is secured and checked on the MWS panel. Engine-driven systems, hydraulic pumps and generators are switched off and, finally, the thrust levers are pulled fully back through the gate in turn to shut down the engines by cutting off the fuel flow. There are a few more actions to shut down the rest of the aircraft systems, including a check on brake temperature before deselecting the brake fans. As soon as the engines have run down, the cabin crew will be opening the front and rear doors ready for the ground steps to be run up to the aircraft. Aircraft and passenger handling at Gatwick is carried out by Gatwick Handling, an independent company partly owned by Dan-Air.

As soon as the steps are in place, the first person aboard the aircraft will be a Traffic Officer from Gatwick Handling who will check that there are no passenger problems which require his immediate attention. The passengers then begin disembarking, being led to the arrival gate by a member of the ground staff while, at the same time, the hold hatches are being opened up to allow the baggage to be offloaded on to the waiting trolleys.

It might be thought that, with the flight completed on schedule and the passengers disembarked, there would be time for the crew to relax before the return leg to Newcastle. However, this is not to be. The time is now 0715 (0815 BST) and the aircraft is due to depart at 0750 as Dan-Air Flight 102. In the next 35min there is a lot of work to be done.

A couple of minutes suffices to round off the paperwork relating to the completed flight, following which the first priority is to calculate the fuel uplift required for the return leg. This is complicated by the fact that the cost of fuel is cheaper at Gatwick than at Newcastle, and so it is company practice to take on enough fuel for both the Gatwick-Newcastle and Newcastle-Bergen flights. The calculated requirement for the flight to Newcastle is 3,760kg and another 2,300kg will be needed for the Bergen sector, making a total requirement of 6,060kg. With 2,500kg remaining on board from the southbound flight, a further uplift of 3,500kg is decided upon. This figure is passed to the Ground Engineer who has come on board to check that all is well with the aircraft; he passes the order on to the driver of the bowser which has drawn up alongside a few minutes after the aircraft's arrival.

While the Captain prepares the navigation log and loadsheet for the next flight, the First Officer leaves the flightdeck for an external check of the aircraft. In the meantime, a party of cleaners has come on board to clear the

Below:

As the passengers disembark, the baggage trolleys are already in position to pick up the bags and freight from the hold. *Dan-Air*

litter from the cabin while the cabin staff help to unload the used meal trays and take on a new batch of hot breakfasts. Following his external check, Andy supervises the refuelling and, having checked the tank gauges and the readings on the bowser, he signs the receipt for the driver and reboards the aircraft.

During a short lull, the two pilots nibble at a crew breakfast which is little more than a glorified sandwich, and take a sip of the ever-available coffee. While doing this the First Officer sorts out the charts which will be required later and files away the used ones.

In the meantime, the passengers for Newcastle will have been checking in at the desk in the departure lounge at Gate 6 and, with 15min to go, the Dispatcher comes aboard with the provisional passenger totals and weights. It looks as if there will be approximately 60 for the return flight and, using this figure, the Captain provisionally completes the load sheet which gives a take-off weight of 33,200kg. Well within the maximum permitted auw, this figure presents no take-off problems due to the length of runway available at Gatwick. Landing weight should be 31,400kg with a fuel burn of 1,800kg — slightly more than the southbound flight due to headwinds on the return leg.

With 10min to go before the scheduled departure time, the chief stewardess reports that the cabin has been cleaned and all meal stocks are on board. With everything proceeding normally, the Captain tells the Dispatcher that the passengers can be allowed to board: a quick call to the departure desk by hand radio and a couple of minutes later they are beginning to come aboard, walking the short distance from the gate and queuing for a moment at the bottom of the steps.

By now the crew are running through the pre-start checks and making the final amendments to the load sheets as the desk advise of one passenger checking in late. The First Officer tunes into 121.75 for the ATIS information to get the departure runway, surface wind, temperature and pressure settings. Predictably, Runway 26 is still in use so the departure will be initially to the west, before turning right through 180° to climb to the north of Gatwick and east of Heathrow then turning north via Airway Blue 4 to Newcastle. In the same way that there are Standard Arrival Procedures (STARs), so also are there Standard Instrument Departure Procedures (SIDs) to cover the initial routeing from Gatwick until clear of the TMA.

With Runway 26 in use, a Daventry 1 SID is most likely and the crew check through this procedure on the chart. Briefly, after take-off the aircraft will climb straight ahead until 1.5 miles west of Gatwick, and then turn right on to a track of 083° towards the Detling VOR which is some 30 miles east-northeast of Gatwick. The aircraft should be at 3,000ft when 23 miles from Detling and 4,000ft at ACORN which is 15 miles short of Detling. At this point it will turn left for point BAKER which is defined as bearing 320° from Detling at a range of 16 miles. Still maintaining 4,000ft, at this point the aircraft will be passing to the east of Heathrow. After BAKER, Dan-Air 102 will turn left on to a track of 320° towards the Brookmans Park radio beacon (NDB) to join the Airway Blue 4. At some time during the SID it is normal for ATC to clear the aircraft to continue its climb to cruising level under radar control, but the exact point at which this will happen depends on the traffic density in the TMA. The crew must therefore make sure that they are fully familiar with the whole procedure in case climb is delayed.

As the last of the passengers are boarding, the First Officer calls Gatwick Delivery on frequency 121.95MHz to request clearance to start. This is the callsign of the Ground Movement Planner who regulates the start-up of departing aircraft in order to control the flow of traffic to the runway. In this way, during busy periods, aircraft can absorb delays waiting on stand rather than sit with engines running for long periods at the holding point to the runway.

First Officer: 'Gatwick Delivery, Dan-Air one zero two on Stand 6 for start-up.'

Gatwick Delivery: 'Dan-Air one zero two, start-up approved. Daventry Departure, Squawk seven four seven seven, contact Ground one two one decimal eight for pushback.'

These instructions are acknowledged and 7477 is set on the Transponder. Cleared to start without delay and, with the doors shut, the First Officer checks on the intercom with the Ground Engineer that the baggage hold doors are shut and all steps and vehicles are clear. Changing to 121.8 (Gatwick Ground) he calls for pushback and permission is duly obtained. The time is 0752, and it is only 45min since arrival at Gatwick as the tractor begins to move the 146 back from Stand 6. Start-up completed, the First Officer calls Ground for taxi clearance:

	G1	LƏ

12 FEB 87

Trans alt **6000**

EGKK

1. Initial climb: Ahead to 700. **2.** Enroute cruising level will be given by 'LONDON Control' after take - off. **3.** Max IAS 250kt below FL 100 unless otherwise authorised. **4.** Emergency R/W 08L/26R - SID designation 08L - W, 26R - V. **5.** Cross noise monitoring points (See C1) not below 1200, thereafter min climb gradient of 4% to 3000 for noise abatement requirements. **6.** 08L Min gradient 5.5% (330'/nm) to 200ft aal (26R not published).

G/S kt	100	130	160	190	220	250	
ft/min	400	520	640	760	880	1000	240'/nm
ft/min	550	720	880	1050	1210	1380	330'/nm

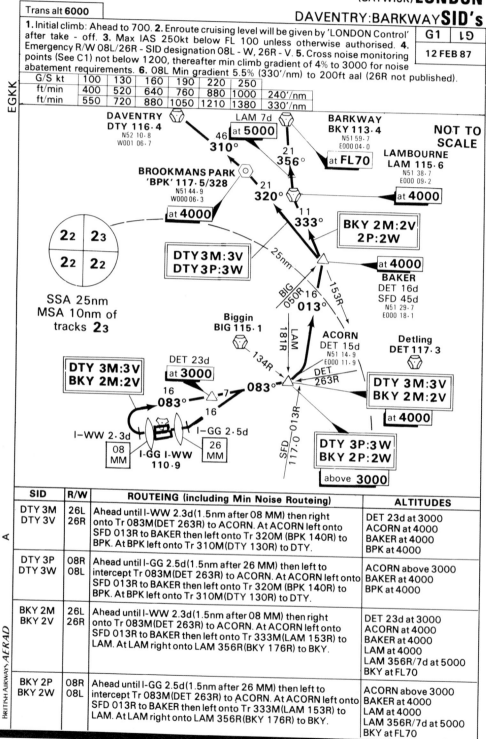

SSA 25nm
MSA 10nm of
tracks **23**

	22	23
	22	22

NOT TO SCALE

I-GG I-WW
110·9

SID	R/W	ROUTEING (including Min Noise Routeing)	ALTITUDES
DTY 3M DTY 3V	26L 26R	Ahead until I-WW 2.3d(1.5nm after 08 MM) then right onto Tr 083M(DET 263R) to ACORN. At ACORN left onto SFD 013R to BAKER then left onto Tr 320M (BPK 140R) to BPK. At BPK left onto Tr 310M(DTY 130R) to DTY.	DET 23d at 3000 ACORN at 4000 BAKER at 4000 BPK at 4000
DTY 3P DTY 3W	08R 08L	Ahead until I-GG 2.5d(1.5nm after 26 MM) then left to intercept Tr 083M(DET 263R) to ACORN. At ACORN left onto SFD 013R to BAKER then left onto Tr 320M (BPK 140R) to BPK. At BPK left onto Tr 310M(DTY 130R) to DTY.	ACORN above 3000 BAKER at 4000 BPK at 4000
BKY 2M BKY 2V	26L 26R	Ahead until I-WW 2.3d(1.5nm after 08 MM) then right onto Tr 083M(DET 263R) to ACORN. At ACORN left onto SFD 013R to BAKER then left onto Tr 333M(LAM 153R) to LAM. At LAM right onto LAM 356R(BKY 176R) to BKY.	DET 23d at 3000 ACORN at 4000 BAKER at 4000 LAM at 4000 LAM 356R/7d at 5000 BKY at FL70
BKY 2P BKY 2W	08R 08L	Ahead until I-GG 2.5d(1.5nm after 26 MM) then left to intercept Tr 083M(DET 263R) to ACORN. At ACORN left onto SFD 013R to BAKER then left onto Tr 333M(LAM 153R) to LAM. At LAM right onto LAM 356R(BKY 176R) to BKY.	ACORN above 3000 BAKER at 4000 LAM at 4000 LAM 356R/7d at 5000 BKY at FL70

A

BRITISH AIRWAYS AERAD

44

First Officer: 'Gatwick Ground, Dan-Air one zero two is ready to taxi.'
Gatwick Ground: :One zero two, taxi to hold alpha, Runway Two Six Left.'

As agreed at the start of the day, the Captain, Peter Hertzberg, will be flying the aircraft on this leg. Opening the throttles slowly he moves the aircraft forward and starts running through the pre-take-off checks: instruments, brakes and trims are all checked and set while both pilots check their ASI bugs set to the correct speeds which have been read off the reference card. In this case these are 112, 115, 128 and 164kt. The navigation aids are set up with the 26ILS (110.9) on NAV1 and Detling VOR on NAV2 for the SID. The rest of the checks are quickly completed and the No 1 stewardess reports the cabin secure for take-off.

It is only a short distance from Stand 6, round the end of the pier to holding point Alpha, alongside the runway threshold.

Gatwick Ground: 'Dan-Air one zero two contact Tower on one two four two two.'

Changing frequency, the First Officer checks in with the Tower:

First Officer: 'Dan-Air one zero two approaching hold Alpha.'

At this time of the morning Gatwick is fairly busy — there are three aircraft holding ahead of the 146 which means a short wait. However, ATC quickly dispatch the others and within a few minutes the aircraft is at the front of the queue.

Gatwick Tower: 'Dan-Air one zero two, after the landing seven three seven line up.'

A Britannia Airways Boeing 737 can be seen to the left with less than a mile to run for landing. As soon as it has passed ahead, the Captain releases the brakes and the 146 moves out on to the runway and turns right through 90° to line up, coming gently to rest as take-off clearance is awaited. The 737 rolls two-thirds of the way down the runway and then clears to

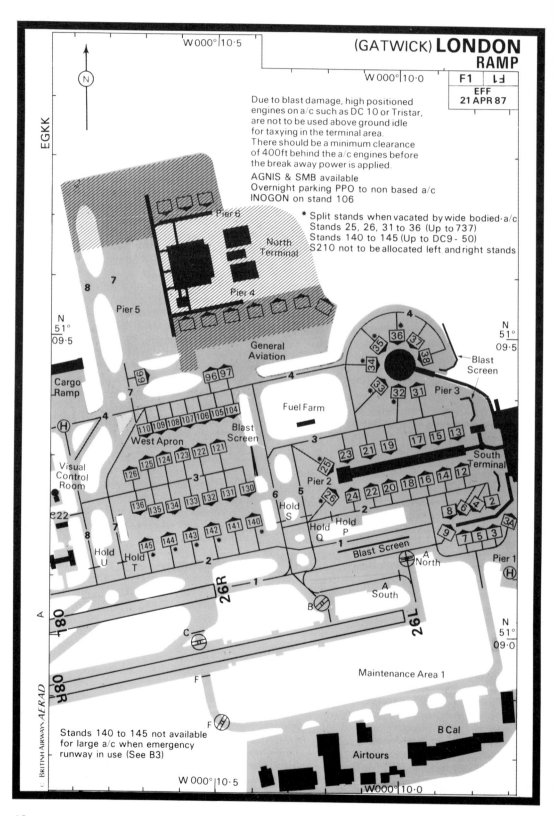

EGKK

Due to blast damage, high positioned
engines on a/c such as DC 10 or Tristar,
are not to be used above ground idle
for taxying in the terminal area.
There should be a minimum clearance
of 400ft behind the a/c engines before
the break away power is applied.

AGNIS & SMB available
Overnight parking PPO to non based a/c
INOGON on stand 106

* Split stands when vacated by wide bodied·a/c
  Stands 25, 26, 31 to 36 (Up to 737)
  Stands 140 to 145 (Up to DC9 - 50)
  S210 not to be allocated left and right stands

Pier 6

North Terminal

Pier 4

Pier 5

General Aviation

Blast Screen

Pier 3

Cargo Ramp

West Apron

Blast Screen

Fuel Farm

Visual Control Room

South Terminal

Pier 2

Hold S

Hold Q

Hold P

Pier 1

Hold U

Hold T

Blast Screen

A North

A South

26R

16L

Maintenance Area 1

B Cal

Airtours

Stands 140 to 145 not available
for large a/c when emergency
runway in use (See B3)

© BRITISH AIRWAYS AERAD

the right as Peter quickly carries out a check of the flying controls and confirms that there are no warnings on the MWS panel.

Gatwick Tower: 'Dan-Air one zero two is cleared for take-off. Wind is three zero zero at one zero knots.'
First Officer: 'Dan-Air one zero two is rolling.'

Pushing the throttle levers fully forward and releasing the brakes, the Captain starts the take-off roll with the First Officer monitoring the instruments and calling the speeds. The aircraft accelerates quickly and, as Andy calls VR (115kt), the control column is eased back and the 146 is airborne again. The undercarriage is quickly retracted and the flaps brought in as speed reaches 155kt and the aircraft climbs through 700ft.

Gatwick Tower: 'Dan-Air one zero two, airborne at zero one. Contact Gatwick Radar on one one eight decimal six.'

By the time the new frequency is selected, the aircraft is through 1,500ft and turning right in accordance with the SID to pick up the 083° radial to the Detling VOR.

First Officer: 'Radar, Dan-Air one zero two passing two thousand feet.'
Gatwick Radar: 'One zero two continue climb to four thousand feet.'

Once settled on course, the 146 is passing only three miles north of Gatwick which can be seen stretching away on the right-hand side. The after take-off checks are completed, the APU shut down and the 'Fasten Seat Belts' sign switched off to allow the cabin crew to start serving another breakfast.

As soon as the Gatwick Radar Controller can see that DA102 is clear of other traffic inbound to the airfield, he hands control over to TMA Southeast, a sector at the London Air Traffic Control Centre. At this stage, apart from an early climb to 4,000ft, the aircraft is still complying with the Daventry SID.

Gatwick Radar: 'Dan-Air one zero two, contact London Control on one two eight decimal four.'

The time is now 0804, only 3min after take-off, but already this is the second frequency change. TMA SE will be responsible for guiding the aircraft through the eastern side of the London TMA before establishing it in a steady climb on Airway Blue 4, routeing up to the Pole Hill VOR, northeast of Manchester.

First Officer: 'London Control, Dan-Air one zero two level at four thousand.'

London Control: 'One zero two report your heading.'

First Officer: 'One zero two is heading zero eight four.'

London Control: 'Dan-Air one zero two turn left, heading zero seven zero, climb to six thousand feet.'

The London controller will do his best to climb the aircraft as soon as possible, bearing in mind the overall traffic situation, since adherence to the SID would entail the 146 remaining at relatively low altitudes until well north of Heathrow, resulting in an uneconomic fuel burn. Already DA102 has been cleared up to an intermediate level and the new heading will cut the corner a bit. Passing abeam Acorn, another heading change is given:

London Control: 'Dan-Air one zero two turn left heading zero one zero.'

The 146 is now passing approximately 20 miles due east of Heathrow and is below aircraft holding at the Lambourne VOR awaiting an approach to land at that airport; such aircraft are normally held at Flight Level 70 or above. As soon as the Controller can see a suitable gap in the traffic flow, he issues a clearance to continue the climb:

Below:
The autopilot control panel is mounted in the glareshield above the Captain's instrument panel. The illuminated arrow symbols show that the autopilot is engaged in the Altitude (ALT) and Heading (HDG) modes.

London Control: 'Dan-Air one zero two, continue climb to Flight Level one zero zero. Turn left, heading three four zero.'

These instructions are complied with, Peter flying the aircraft on the autopilot using the HDG and VS modes, and adjusting the Altitude Selector as successive climb clearances are passed.

In the meantime the First Officer, in consultation with the Captain, is selecting and monitoring a succession of frequency changes on the navigation equipment. After departure, Detling is on NAV1 and Lambourne on NAV2 so that the SID procedure can be flown. Also selected is the Brookmans Park NDB which is just over 20 miles northeast of Heathrow and

Below:
ATC clear DA102 direct to Pole Hill and the First Officer checks his radio navigation chart for the correct track to follow.

marks the beginning of Airway Blue 4. The NDB frequency (328kHz) is set on ADF1 and the bearings generated can be fed through to the HSD pointers instead of one of the VORs, if desired. Once the initial legs of the SID have been flown and the aircraft is under radar control, then the First Officer selects Daventry (116.4MHz) on NAV1 and, a little later, Pole Hill (112.1MHz) on NAV2.

Passing just to the west of Lambourne, the 146 is beginning to come clear of the TMA traffic and further climb is forthcoming:

London Control: 'Dan-Air one zero two continue climb to Flight level one seven zero, contact London Control on one two five decimal eight.'

The First Officer acknowledges, changes frequency, and calls up:

First Officer: 'London Control, Dan-Air one zero two heading three four zero, cleared one seven zero.'
London Control: 'Dan-Air one zero two turn left, heading three three zero.'

It is now 0815, 14min after take-off, and DA102 is becoming established on Airway Blue 4 which is on the eastern side of the main north-south airways system running the length of the country. Between London and Manchester, southbound traffic is routed down the western side of this system using Airways Amber 1 and Amber 1 East, while northbound flights are routed on Airways Amber 2 and Blue 4. This one-way flow system reduces the likelihood of a confrontation between outbound aircraft climbing and inbound aircraft which are descending. Once on course and north of the TMA, clearance to continue the climb to the requested cruising level of Flight Level 280 is quickly given:

London Control: 'Dan-Air one zero two, climb to Flight Level two eight zero, cleared own navigation direct to Pole Hill.'

The call is acknowledged and the Captain selects the V/L mode on the autopilot, slaving it to the Pole Hill VOR. In this mode the autopilot will keep the aircraft on a selected bearing so that it will track directly towards the VOR. The readout from Pole Hill shows that a track of 334° is needed and this is set up on the Course Selector to the right of the Autopilot Mode Selector. 28,000ft is wound on to the Altitude Selector and rate of climb adjusted to maintain 280kt.

As the workload of flying the aircraft decreases now that it is clear of the busiest airspace, there is now time for other tasks. The Captain calls Dan-Air Operations at Gatwick to confirm the flight's progress:

Captain: 'Dan Ops, Mike November with 61 passengers and 216kg of freight for Newcastle. Off chocks at fifty two, airborne at zero one, on chocks at Newcastle on the hour.'

This message is acknowledged by Operations who will record this information and, in turn, pass it on by teleprinter to the airline's traffic office at Newcastle so that the necessary preparations to receive the flight can be made.

Back aboard the 146 the crew are monitoring the climb to cruising level. The leg from the Brookmans Park NDB to the Pole Hill VOR is 140 miles and should take 22min. By the time the aircraft is over Nottingham, it is levelling at Flight Level 280 having taken a total of 21min in the climb due to the restrictions in the London TMA. The First Officer selects London Volmet (North) on 126.60MHz where he can listen in to the weather reports for the northern UK airfields, including Newcastle. According to the forecasts, there should have been little change in conditions at Newcastle since departure from there nearly two-and-a-half hours ago. The weather reports are actually given out by a computer generated voice of surprisingly good quality:

London Volmet: ' . . . Newcastle at zero seven five zero, two eight zero degrees one zero knots, ten kilometres or more, three OKTA at two five zero zero, temperature plus one four, dew point plus one zero, QNH One zero two two, NOSIG . . . Glasgow at zero seven . . .'

The transmission is continuous and, having obtained the weather reports for Newcastle and the diversion airfields at Edinburgh and Teesside, Peter switches back to the ATC frequency. He is just in time to hear the First Officer acknowledging an instruction to change to London Control on 131.05MHz, having already reported that the aircraft is level at Flight Level 280. This is the Pole Hill sector which will look after the flight until it leaves the Airways system five miles northeast of the Pole Hill VOR.

Peter continues with a routine check of the fuel state, plotting fuel remaining against the requirements to safely complete the flight. The headwinds appear to be less than forecast and the aircraft is making up time with a consequent slight fuel saving. This is also a

Left:
**The northbound route follows Airway Blue 4 to
the Pole Hill VOR.** *AERAD*

good time to inform the passengers of the
progress of the flight and he does this on the
cabin PA system, pointing out places of
interest visible below the aircraft, confirming
that the Newcastle weather is good, and giving
the good news that the flight is slightly ahead
of schedule. A stewardess comes forward with
two more cups of coffee and the crew have a
few minutes to relax and chat while keeping a
listening watch on the ATC frequency.

However, this lull does not last long and,
with 25 miles to run to Pole Hill, it is time to
start descent although clearance must first be
obtained from ATC:

First Officer: 'London, Dan-Air one zero two is
ready for descent.'
London Control: 'Dan-Air one zero two,
descend to Flight Level two two zero.'

With permission given, Peter starts easing the
aircraft down, slightly reducing the power and
setting up the autopilot for descent to 22,000ft.
The start of the descent does not pass
unnoticed by the cabin crew who know that
they now have approximately 15min to clear
up the meal trays and coffee cups, and secure
the cabin for landing.

The navigation aids are now set up with
Newcastle VOR (113.5MHz) on NAV1 while
Pole Hill is left on NAV2. The latter is crossed
at time 0736 and the Captain turns on to a
heading of due north by altering the heading
bug to 360° and selecting HDG mode instead of
V/L on the autopilot. ATC is advised of this:

First Officer: 'Dan-Air one zero two is Pole
Hill at three six, passing two four zero.
Newcastle at five zero.'
London Control: 'Dan-Air one zero two
continue descent to Flight Level one one zero,
Squawk one four zero one, contact Border
Radar on one three two decimal nine.'

The leg between Pole Hill and Newcastle is
outside the controlled airspace of the airways
system, consequently the ATC services have
set up a unit at RAF Boulmer in Northumber-
land to provide a radar service to aircraft en
route over the northeast of England; these are
civil controllers, but use the military radar
equipment to do their job. The early morning
outbound flight from Newcastle was not
controlled by this unit as the service provided
does not commence until 0630 each morning.
The First Officer checks in on 132.9:

First Officer: 'Border Radar, Dan-Air one zero
two is off the Pole descending to Level one one
zero on track to GATER.'
Border Radar: 'Dan-Air one zero two, Squawk
Ident, turn right heading zero two zero, no
delay for Runway two five at Newcastle.'

The normal routeing from Pole Hill to
Newcastle is via GATER, which is a VOR
intersection 25 miles southwest of Newcastle
VOR, in order to pass to the west of the Vale of
York where there is often intensive military
flying training in progress. However, the area
is quiet today and the Border controller takes
advantage of this to give DA102 a direct route
to its destination. He will also be in telephone
communication with Newcastle Approach
Control and will have obtained a safe level for
further descent from them, together with a
new squawk. With the aircraft observed to be
approaching Flight Level 110 and some 35
miles south of Newcastle, he issues
instructions to effect a transfer of control to
the airfield:

Border Radar: 'Dan-Air one zero two continue
descent to Flight Level seven zero, Squawk
seven two four two, contact Newcastle Radar
on one two six decimal three five.'

The call is acknowledged, the new squawk and
frequency selected, autopilot adjusted and
contact established with Newcastle.

First Officer: 'Newcastle Radar, Dan-Air one
zero two is three five miles south, passing
Flight Level one one zero, heading zero two
zero.'
Newcastle Radar: 'Dan-Air one zero two,
Squawk Ident, expect radar vectoring to ILS
approach Runway two five.'

The First Officer presses the Ident button on
the Transponder, causing a flashing symbol
alongside the aircraft's blip on the radar
screen. With the 146 positively identified the
controller issues further instructions:

Newcastle Radar: 'Dan-Air one zero two is
identified at three two miles south of Newcastle. Turn right heading zero three zero and
continue descent to Flight Level three five.'
First Officer: 'One zero two is cleared to three
five, turning right zero three zero.'

On passing Flight Level 100, the descent and
approach checks are run through and the ASI
and N1 bugs are set. The First Officer selects
111.5MHz on NAV2 and listens in to the

Above:
The River Tyne and its spectacular bridges provide a clear fix for a visual approach.

associated Morse code signal to confirm that the ILS for Runway 25 is transmitting correctly.

The Newcastle Radar controller then passes the current weather report for the airfield, the details of which do not differ from the earlier report received from the VOLMET transmission.

At 20 miles south of the airfield, the 146 is passing Flight Level 60 and now the Captain reduces power slightly to start bringing the speed back to 250kt. The aircraft is passing through a broken cloud layer and, although the ground below is in sight, forward visibility is limited. The final approach checks are completed. APU 'on', brake fans 'on', fuel pumps selected and 'on'. The No 1 opens the flightdeck door and reports that the cabin is secured for landing. Radar calls again:

Newcastle Radar: 'Dan-Air one zero two is one three miles south-southeast of the field approaching a base leg to the ILS. You are number two in traffic. Maintain three five on reaching.'

In accordance with these instructions, Peter levels off the 146 as Flight Level 35 is reached, observing that the aircraft is still just above the cloud base. The aircraft ahead is a Boeing 737 inbound from Heathrow and can be heard reporting established on the ILS. One minute later, ATC calls again:

Newcastle Radar: 'Dan-Air one zero two descend to two five zero zero feet on QNH one zero two two. You are one zero miles southeast of the field.'

The Captain complies with this and continues to reduce speed still further, aiming for 210kt. His target threshold speed (V ref) is 109kt, read from the reference card which has been turned over to show the speeds appropriate to the landing weight of 31,000kg.

On passing 2,800ft, the First Officer calls that he has the airfield in sight away on the port side. The Captain glances in the indicated direction, confirms that he also can see the runway and both pilots scan the approach area looking for the Boeing 737 ahead. It is quickly spotted on a short final, about five or six miles ahead of the 146. The First Officer calls ATC:

First Officer: 'Dan-Air one zero two has the airfield and number one in sight. Request visual approach.'
Newcastle Radar: 'Dan-Air one zero two is cleared for visual approach. Report on final, QFE threshold Runway two five is one zero one two.'

Given suitable weather and traffic conditions, most crews prefer to make a visual approach wherever possible in order to save a little time and as a change from the standard ILS. The First Officer continues to monitor the ILS indications and altitude as the Captain further reduces speed, helped by judicious use of the airbrake, to come down to 170kt on base leg. He also disconnects the autopilot and concentrates on flying the aircraft manually. The QFE is set on the Captain's altimeter while the First Officer's remains on QNH. Cabin air is selected from the APU and engine bleed air is shut off.

Peter calls for 18° of flap as he initiates the turn on to final approach at six miles from touchdown. This is quickly followed by a call for the undercarriage and Andy operates the lever, confirming when a satisfactory row of green lights appears to indicate that the wheels are down and locked.

First Officer: 'Dan-Air one zero two on finals.'
Newcastle Radar: 'One zero two continue

approach, contact Newcastle Tower one one nine decimal seven.'

Peter acknowledges and then calls for the next stage of flap (24°) before changing to the Tower frequency:

First Officer: 'Newcastle Tower, Dan-Air one zero two is on finals at four miles.'
Newcastle Tower: 'One zero two, continue approach.'

The 737 which has just landed can be seen turning off the runway and as soon as it is clear, landing clearance is forthcoming:

Newcastle Tower: 'One zero two is cleared to land. Surface wind two nine zero at one zero knots.'
First Officer: 'One zero two is cleared to land.'

With flaps and wheels down the speed is reducing nicely, and presently shows 145kt. As the runway approaches, the Captain successively calls for 30° and then 33° of flap and crosses the threshold spot on the target 109kt with the airbrake fully extended; a gentle flare and there is the satisfying feel of a gentle touchdown. Immediately he calls 'spoilers' and 'engines to ground idle', and Andy quickly executes these commands. Aiming for the turn-off to the right two-thirds of the way down the runway, calls for firm braking and the aircraft's speed quickly falls to 40kt. The airbrakes and spoilers are retracted and the flaps raised as the 146 turns off the runway and the Tower issues the taxying instructions:

Newcastle Tower: 'One zero two landed at five two. Vacate the runway on the right, park on Stand Two.'

Since the aircraft will be carrying on to Bergen later in the morning, it is necessary to allocate it to one of the Customs stands ranged along the south side of the pier, the opposite side to which it was parked at the start of the day. Steering now with the nosewheel tiller, the Captain guides the aircraft slowly on to the designated parking area, following the yellow

Right:
Short finals for Runway 25. The pilot is aiming to touchdown about 1,000ft past the striped markings which denote the beginning of the landing threshold.

Below:
The BAe146 touches down at Newcastle with the airbrakes fully extended.

guidelines painted on the apron surface. As he brakes gently to a stop the service vehicles and mobile steps are waiting, ready to move quickly into position as the engines are shut down.

Pulling up at the indicated stop bar, the crew quickly run through the shutdown checks — brakes 'on' and checked, flightdeck window opened to confirm cabin depressurised, hydraulic pumps 'off', generators 'off', engines 'shut down' seat belts sign 'off', brake fans 'off' after checking brake temperature, fuel pumps 'off', heaters 'off', ice detectors 'off', flashing beacon light 'off'.

While these checks are being completed, the cabin crew have opened the doors as soon as the engines were shut down and the steps are already in place. A member of the groundstaff waits to lead the passengers to the terminal as they begin to disembark. In the meantime the pilots finish off the paperwork, noting the fuel used on the flight and entering this and the total remaining in the technical log. Also recorded are the peak EGTs when starting which had been jotted down on the navigation log when at Gatwick. The First Officer refiles the charts which have been used and stows away the various manuals in the pockets beside the seats.

An engineer comes on board to see if there are any new snags on the aircraft, but Peter is able to assure him that all is well. However, he stays on board and checks through the technical log before inspecting the aircraft prior to the next departure, due in an hour-and-a-half.

With all checks complete, Peter and Andy collect their bags and walk down the steps on to the tarmac, leaving the aircraft to the army of cleaners, caterers, engineers and baggage handlers as they ready the aircraft for the next flight. The time is now 0915 (1015 BST), just over 20min after landing and 4hr 15min since they first arrived at Newcastle Airport to start planning for the day's flights to and from Gatwick. Although they have the rest of the day free, both face a busy weekend ahead and will be glad of the break.

In the meantime, there is no rest for the aircraft as the next crew prepare for the flight across the North Sea to Norway and return.

Below:

Taxying in to park on Stand 2 — straight ahead is the control tower with the main terminal on the right.

Bottom:

During the turnaround between flights, an Engineer checks the technical log before inspecting the aircraft.

Across the North Sea

In contrast to the crew of Dan-Air 101/102, Captain Stuart Burns has been able to rise at a civilised hour and take a relaxed breakfast before setting off for Newcastle Airport where he arrives just after 1000 (BST). Today he is rostered to take Mike November on the daily scheduled flight to Bergen in Norway, returning to Newcastle via Stavanger. Bergen is an important port on the west coast of Norway and is the base for many ferry operations to the country's northern ports and cities. Stavanger is also a port and is heavily involved in supporting Norway's offshore oil industry. The Dan-Air scheduled flights are much used by the business communities of both countries as well as holidaymakers eager to explore the magnificent scenery of the Norwegian fjords and mountains. In the opposite direction there is a steady stream of Norwegians anxious to take advantage of the shopping facilities offered by Newcastle: one spree in Marks & Spencer's can often save more than the cost of the air fare, given the high price of consumer items in Scandinavia.

However, Captain Burns has other matters on his mind as he arrives at the airport and makes his way to the traffic office. Achieving an on-time departure for Flight DA846 is subject to two factors which are entirely outside his control: for a start he is dependent on the arrival of the inbound DA102 from Gatwick reasonably on schedule. It is due at 0900 (1000 BST) and DA846 is scheduled to depart at 1035 (1135 BST) which gives approximately 1½hr for the turnaround and provides some latitude if 102 is slightly delayed. However, a major delay due to technical problems or disruptions at Gatwick caused by traffic congestion or bad weather will cause the Bergen flight to run late.

The other factor is that the operation of DA846 is closely linked with another flight, DA842, which originates at Manchester and comes through Newcastle to Oslo, completing the airline's route structure to Norway. Passengers from Manchester wishing to travel to Bergen and Stavanger change aircraft on arrival at Newcastle, while some travelling from Gatwick to Oslo will also change at Newcastle, although the latter are less common as Dan-Air also operate a direct Gatwick-Oslo flight. However, the result is that DA846 cannot depart until DA842 has arrived from Manchester and any transfer passengers have been boarded. This flight is not due until 1020 (1120 BST), so the margin here is narrow.

Captain Burns' first actions, therefore, are to check on the status of the Gatwick and Manchester flights. In fact DA102 has already landed and, at the moment, it appears that DA842 should be operating on schedule, although it is not due to leave Manchester for another 45min. The Captain's briefing sheet informs him that handling at Bergen and Stavanger, as usual, will be carried out by Braathens SAFE (the Norwegian domestic airline) and gives the necessary addresses, telephone and telex numbers.

Walking over to the flight planning office, he meets his First Officer, Cliff Newton, who is already gathering the weather information for the flight. The procedures followed are parallel to those of the earlier crew planning the Gatwick route. A check of the NOTAMS reveals that one of Stavanger's runways may be closed for maintenance, but as it is not the main instrument runway this should cause no problems. However, the weather is not so kind: the relatively clear conditions during the morning have followed the passage of a cold

front over the British Isles; this front is now situated over the eastern North Sea leaving the west coast of Norway under a layer of cloud with some rain. The current weather report for Bergen gives a light southwesterly wind, a visibility of 10km, and a main cloud base of 1,800ft although there are patches below; temperature is a mild 13°C. Stavanger is slightly worse with a main cloud base of 1,000ft and some rain. The forecasts indicate that these conditions will prevail and possibly worsen slightly, although not to such an extent that it will be impossible to make an approach and landing at either airfield. The upper winds are generally westerly, becoming southerly over Norway giving a favourable 21kt tailwind component on the outbound leg, although this will convert to a 27kt headwind component on the return from Stavanger.

Taking these figures, the Estimated Elapsed Time (EET) for the flight to Bergen is calculated as 69min. Bergen to Stavanger will take 20min, and the return to Newcastle 70min. The latter leg is actually 50 miles shorter than the outbound sector but will take slightly longer due to the headwinds.

Using these figures, the total fuel requirement for the Newcastle-Bergen sector works out at 4,275kg including the reserves to divert to Stavanger if required. Cliff makes a quick check and finds that the aircraft, which is now parked on the apron with all passengers and crew disembarked from the Gatwick flight, still has 4,800kg of fuel on board. As this is slightly in excess of the requirements, there is no need to arrange any refuelling.

By 0950 the planning is complete and the crew walk out to the aircraft which is a hive of activity: a party of cleaners has given the cabin a thorough going-over and are gathering up their equipment. On the starboad side meal trays are being loaded into the galley while one of the cabin crew is carrying out an inventory of the duty-free bar. In the cockpit an Engineer is checking the technical log and bringing some of the records up to date.

After stowing their bags, the First Officer carries out the standard external check of the aircraft while the Captain talks with the engineer before signing the technical log. Both pilots then settle down to the routine preparation for the flight. Cliff calls Newcastle Tower for the airfield data and is informed that the wind is westerly at 10kt, temperature is 16°C, QNH is 1023mb and QFE for Runway 25 is 1013mb. After consulting the performance manual, he sets the bugs on the engine N1 gauges for take-off power. He then selects the charts for the flight and consults with the Captain over the noise abatement procedure to be followed. After departure, the aircraft will settle on to a course of 041° (roughly northeast) which would normally require a right turn out from Runway 25. However, the Minimum Noise Routeing requires that the aircraft should maintain a westerly heading for four miles after take-off before turning right on course. On the other hand, if a left turn out is possible then it is only necessary to pass 1,000ft in the climb before starting a turn. It will be quicker to do this, coming back over the airfield to set course, so the crew decide to ask for this departure.

Having made these decisions Captain Burns, who will be flying the aircraft on this leg, carries out his departure and safety briefing as the passengers are beginning to board. The latter are accompanied by the dispatcher who has the up-to-date load sheet and confirms the total load as 25 males, 35 females, and 18 children. Total payload, including baggage and cargo, comes to 6,871kg and take-off weight is just under 34,500kg. Cliff therefore sets the reference card to this figure and clips it in place.

As the passengers board, a problem becomes apparent: it appears that most of the 18 children are members of a Norwegian youth band who have been touring Northeast England and included in their baggage is a large selection of musical instruments in cases. Several of these will not fit into the hold and the loaders ask if some can be carried in the cabin. After some deliberation the Captain, conscious of the need to keep the cabin free of obstructions in case of an emergency, gives permission for this provided they are safely stowed on unoccupied seats.

The flight from Manchester has arrived on schedule and is parked alongside. As soon as the engines are shut down, passengers for Bergen are disembarked and conducted across the apron to the waiting 146. With the final formalities completed the ground staff withdraw, doors are shut, and the First Officer checks with the engineer on the external intercom that he is ready for pushback. The Engineer confirms that the tractor is coupled up and all vehicles are clear of the aircraft. Clearance to push is then requested.

First Officer: 'Newcastle Tower, Dan-Air eight four six is ready for start on Stand Two.'
Newcastle Tower: 'Dan-Air eight four six, pushback and start approved. Temperature is one six.'

Below:
Passengers for Bergen and Stavanger board the aircraft.

He signals to the Ground Engineer and the tractor smoothly moves the aircraft back off the stand ready for starting engines. These are quickly run up, peak TGTs being noted for the log, and the First Officer calls for taxi clearance:

First Officer: 'Tower, Dan-Air eight four six request taxi clearance.'
Newcastle Tower: 'Dan-Air eight four six taxi to hold Bravo for Runway two five. QNH is one zero two three.'

As the aircraft begins to move forward the cabin crew report that the cabin is secure for take-off and the pilots begin the pre-take-off checks. Approaching the holding point, ATC clear the 146 to enter the runway:

Newcastle Tower: 'Dan-Air eight four six, enter, backtrack and line up Runway two five.'
First Officer: 'Eight four six Roger. We are requesting a left turn out after departure.'
Newcastle Tower: 'Roger eight four six. Your departure instructions are to make a left turn after noise abatement. Maintain Flight Level six five, further climb when instructed by radar, Squawk one four zero four.'
First Officer: 'Eight four six is cleared left turn out. Maintain six five. Squawk one four zero four.'

With this exchange complete, the aircraft is now on the runway, taxying to the eastern end to line up for take-off. The pre-take-off checks continue — flaps, instruments, trims, TMS, configuration, nav aids, transponder, cabin secure, continuous ignition, controls, strobes, lights, clear MWS panel. Checks completed as the aircraft turns at the end of the runway, the Captain asks Cliff to obtain take-off clearance. This is immediately forthcoming from the tower and the thrust levers are moved fully forward, brakes released and Mike November starts its third take-off of the day.

With 18° of flap set VR is 117kt and V2 129kt, and these speeds are quickly passed as the aircraft lifts off at 1048. Flaps up passing 700ft and at 1,000ft Captain Burns banks over into a wide left turn to bring the aircraft on to the required track of 041°. Power is increased for the climb and, with a rate of 2,000ft/min established, the VS lock is selected on the autopilot together with the HDG lock. The Captain adjusts the HSD bug to keep the turn going and settles back to monitor the climb.

Newcastle Tower: 'Dan-Air eight four six airborne at four eight. Contact Newcastle Radar one two six three five.'

This call is acknowledged and both pilots switch to the new frequency.

First Officer: 'Radar, eight four six is passing two thousand feet turning left.'
Newcastle Radar: 'Dan-Air eight four six report approaching Flight Level six zero.'

Climb checks are completed and the APU is shut down as the aircraft passes 4,500ft. Both altimeters are now set to 1013mb to read standard flight levels and already the aircraft is approaching Flight Level 60:

First Officer: 'Dan-Air eight four six passing five five for six zero.'
Newcastle Radar: 'Eight four six continue climb to Flight Level two three zero.'

The Autopilot Altitude Selector is wound round to read 23,000 and the rate of climb reduced to 1,500ft/min to allow the speed to increase slightly. The 146 is normally restricted to a speed of 250kt (IAS) until passing Flight Level 80 when 280kt or Mach 0.6 is maintained in the climb.

Below:
Reference speeds are displayed for landing at Newcastle; threshold target speed will be 112kt. On the right is the TMS control panel — the CTRL button has been selected and shows N1 which indicates that on application of full power the engines will automatically run up to the N1 figure selected on the N1 gauge bug. If TGT was selected then the engines would run up such that a temperature of 840°C, as set on the panel, would be the limiting factor.

Left:
The Captain adjusts the heading bug on the HSD to keep the aircraft in the left turn to bring it on to a track of 041°.

Although only 5min after take-off, the 146 is passing 8,000ft and has crossed the coast just to the northeast of Newcastle. From this point the rest of the route is entirely over the North Sea, except for the landfall and final approach to Bergen. A straight line track is normally followed unless there is a major military air exercise in progress, in which case a detour north of the direct route is sometimes necessary.

Apart from the VOR at Newcastle and the Flesland VOR at Bergen, there are no other navigation aids along the aircraft's track. However, the VORs at Aberdeen and Sola (Stavanger) are used for cross-bearings and to give an indication of progress along the track. On departure, NAV1 and NAV2 are both set to 113.5 for the Newcastle VOR, but as the climb continues NAV1 is changed to 114.3 to pick up the Aberdeen VOR. Once out over the sea, control of the aircraft is transferred to Border Radar:

Newcastle Radar: 'Dan-Air eight four six contact Border Radar on one three four decimal eight five.'

Changing to the new frequency, the First Officer checks in:

First Officer: 'Border Radar, Dan-Air eight four six is passing Flight Level one zero zero, requesting two nine zero.'
Border Radar: 'Roger eight four six. Squawk Ident.'

The First Officer presses the Ident button on the Transponder. With the aircraft identity confirmed, the controller is able to issue a clearance to continue the climb:

Border Radar: 'Dan-Air eight four six is identified at three zero miles northeast of Newcastle. Continue climb to Flight Level two nine zero.'

A few minutes later there is another call:

Border Radar: 'Eight four six, Border, what is your estimate for the FIR boundary?'

The First Officer checks the navigation log and replies:

First Officer: 'Eight four six estimates the boundary at three zero.'

The FIR boundary in this case is the division between the airspace of the Scottish Air Traffic Control Centre and the area under control of the Stavanger ATCC, and is approximately two-thirds of the way across to Bergen. At that point, control of the aircraft will be taken over by Norwegian controllers at Stavanger. In the meantime, the aircraft has reached Flight Level 290 at 1106, 18min after take-off and is now approximately 100 miles southeast of Aberdeen.

In level flight the power settings are adjusted to give the optimum cruising speed. Reading from performance tables which take into account the altitude, outside air temperature (minus 28°C) and aircraft weight, the First Officer comes up with the figure of Mach 0.68. This equates to an IAS of 256kt which, in turn, is equivalent to a TAS of 400kt.

With the aircraft settled in the cruise, the Captain next turns his attention to obtaining

Above:
Rate of climb is now 1,500ft/min as the BAe146 climbs through 16,000ft.

the latest weather reports for both Bergen and Stavanger. Both these airfields transmit continuous reports and terminal information on a separate ATIS frequency, Bergen on 125.25MHz and Stavanger on 126.0MHz. Selecting each in turn, he records the data transmitted on the navigation logsheet. Stavanger is giving a surface wind of 300° at 7kt, visibility 9km, cloud cover of two oktas at 900ft and five oktas at 1,500ft, temperature 16°C and QNH 1014. Bergen is similar, with a wind of 250° at 5kt, visibility 10km, two oktas at 1,000ft and six oktas at 1,500ft, temperature 15°C and QNH 1014. The ILS for Runway 18 is in use at Bergen. Both reports are similar to the forecast conditions and will present no problems for the approach and landing.

With the weather information to hand, the Captain now talks to the passengers passing on the usual information regarding the progress of the flight and conditions at Bergen. As they listen, the passengers will be enjoying a light lunch with wine which is served on this flight.

At 1113 the flightdeck routine is interrupted by a call from Border Radar:

Border Radar: 'Dan-Air eight four six, contact Highland Radar on one three four decimal zero.'

The call is acknowledged and the new frequency quickly selected.

Captain: 'Highland Radar, Dan-Air eight four six, level at two nine zero.'
Highland Radar: 'Dan-Air eight four six, Highland Radar, Squawk zero six four two.'

The new code is selected on the Transponder,

triggering a further call from the Radar controller:

Highland Radar: 'Dan-Air eight four six is identified one hundred miles east of Aberdeen, report at the FIR boundary.'

Highland Radar is, like Border Radar, a civil ATC unit using the military radars to provide a service to aircraft flying over the North Sea. To illustrate the variety of traffic, a couple of helicopters flying to North Sea oil rigs from Aberdeen can also be heard on the frequency.

The Captain continues his paperwork, this time with a look at the fuel state which checks out normally. The First Officer sorts out the landing charts for Bergen and, after checking the procedures for the ILS on Runway 18, sets up the various navigation aids. There are two NDBs associated with this procedure, the BM (Bravo Mike) on 374kHz which is a low-powered locator beacon situated on runway centreline half-a-mile from touchdown, and the ASK (Alpha Sierra Kilo) on 360kHz which is seven miles north of the airfield but still on the runway centreline. There are no STAR procedures at Bergen for aircraft arriving from the west, but it is anticipated that the initial inbound clearance will be to the ASK. The ASK frequency is set on ADF1 and BM on ADF2, although both are much too far away to be picked up at this stage. Navigation is still by means of the VORs and the Newcastle VOR on NAV2 shows that the aircraft is presently (the time now being 1117) 176 miles on a bearing of 042° from the departure point. However, this is beginning to draw out of range and so NAV1 has been switched to 114.5 to pick up the Flesland VOR situated on the airfield at Bergen. Initially this, too, is out of range and a flag appears on the HSD to indicate that a strong enough signal is not being received, but after a couple of minutes it is reading normally. By 1125 the DME shows a distance of 150.8 miles to Bergen, about 22min flying time at the present speed. NAV2 is then selected to 114.2MHz to pick up the SOLA VOR at Stavanger. Bearings from this will give a good check of the aircraft's position along its track to the Flesland VOR.

By 1128 the DME is showing 130 miles to run to Bergen which indicates that the aircraft is crossing the FIR boundary, and this information is passed to ATC:

Right:
Radio navigation chart covering the North Sea between Scotland and Norway. *AERAD*

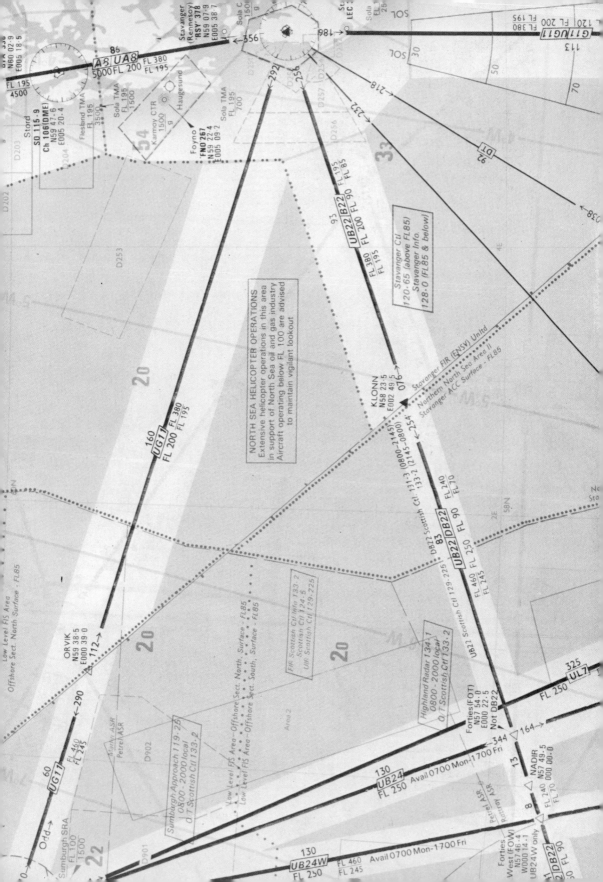

NORTH SEA HELICOPTER OPERATIONS
Extensive helicopter operations in this area
in support of North Sea oil and gas industry.
Aircraft operating below FL 100 are advised
to maintain vigilant lookout

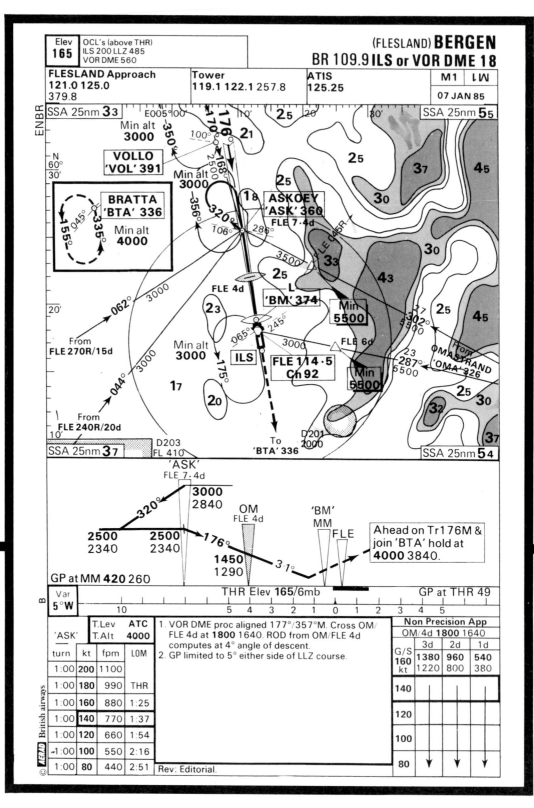

First Officer: 'Highland Radar, Dan-Air eight four six is the boundary at two eight '
Highland Radar: 'Roger Dan-Air eight four six, contact Stavanger Control to one two four decimal seven.'

Another quick change of frequency:

First Officer: 'Stavanger Control, Dan-Air eight four six is the FIR boundary at two eight, Flight Level two nine zero, Bergen at five zero, requesting descent.'
Stavanger Control: 'Dan-Air eight four six is cleared to Flight Level one six zero, Squawk four two seven six.'
First Officer: 'Eight four six is leaving Flight Level two nine zero, Squawk is four two seven six.'

With this exchange completed, Captain Burns sets the aircraft up for descent. 16,000ft is wound on to the Autopilot Selector and power is reduced to give readings of 85% N1, 86% N2 and a TGT of 670°C. Fuel flow is reduced from 500kg/hr for each engine in the cruise, to 380kg/hr; and at the top of descent the total fuel used since take off is 1,960kg. With the reduction in power a rate of descent of around 1,200ft/min is established and the VS mode selected on the autopilot. Standard descent checks are commenced and, as the 146 passes Flight Level 255 in the descent, it enters into the top of a high cloud layer associated with the worsening weather on this side of the North Sea.

Stavanger Control can be heard clearing another aircraft, Scandinavian 931, to descend to Level 290 which the 146 has just left. The First Officer selects the ATIS on 125.25MHz to get an update on the latest weather at Bergen and this indicates that there has been no change; this is information 'November', updated at 1120.

With 50 miles to run, Stavanger hand the aircraft over to the ATC unit at Bergen, callsign Flesland Radar:

Stavanger Control: 'Dan-Air eight four six is cleared to Flight Level one zero zero, contact Flesland Radar on one two one decimal zero.'

These instructions are acknowledged and complied with, and descent continued as cleared:

First Officer: 'Flesland Radar, Dan-Air eight four six is a one four six with November, descending to Flight Level one zero zero.'
Flesland Radar: 'Roger eight four six, continue descent to Flight Level eight zero.'

Further descent! Things are looking good.

Flesland Radar: 'Eight four six this will be radar vectoring to the ILS for Runway one eight, you are number three in traffic.'

Ah well, it couldn't last! Ahead can be heard a couple of SAS aircraft also being positioned on to the ILS. Interestingly, the Controller can also be heard clearing a Dan-Air eight three three to climb to two eight zero. This will be a company BAC One-Eleven operating the direct flight from Bergen to Gatwick, having made the outbound flight earlier in the morning.

On the 146, descent checks are complete and the crew are running through the approach checks. Cliff has turned NAV2 to the ILS

Far left:
The ILS approach chart for Bergen. *AERAD*

Left:
35 miles to run and the Captain prepares for an ILS approach to Runway 18 with the appropriate chart clipped to the control column. The Flesland VOR (114.5MHz) is selected on the NAV1 set.

frequency 109.9MHz and checked the coding. At 1143, with the aircraft now some 20 miles southwest of Bergen, radar takes full control of the flight to fit it into the traffic sequence:

Flesland Radar: 'Dan-Air eight four six turn left, heading zero two zero, continue descent to four thousand feet on QNH one zero one four.'

This instruction is acknowledged, both pilots having already set 1014mb on their altimeters as part of the descent checks. Both NAV sets are now on the ILS frequency while the two beacons (BM and ASK) are switched through to the pointers on the HSD. A couple of minutes later there is another call:

Flesland Radar: 'Dan-Air eight four six is cleared to three thousand feet on QNH.'

By 1147 the aircraft is level at 3,000ft and is just on top of a layer of cloud. The First Officer reports reaching the assigned altitude:

First Officer: 'Flesland Radar, Dan-Air eight four six is level at three thousand feet.'
Flesland Radar: 'Roger eight four six, turn right heading one two zero.'

The Captain complies with this instruction and, as the aircraft turns towards the ILS, he concentrates on reducing speed which is already less than 250kt. As soon as he is steady on the new heading there are further instructions:

Flesland Radar: 'Dan-Air eight four six turn right heading one four zero degrees and descend to two five zero zero feet. Closing the ILS from the right, report established. QFE is one zero zero eight.'

Again, these instructions are complied with and the Captain sets his altimeter to QFE and checks the difference in readings with the First Officer's altimeter which remains set on QNH. The aircraft is now 10 miles from touchdown,

Left:
Short final: the runway at Bergen is not flat, as this view shows.

approaching the ILS Localiser at a closing
angle of some 40°; the autopilot is set in the
GLS mode for an automatic lock-on. The cabin
has been reported as secure for landing and
the APU is on and running. Speed is reducing
to 180kt as the Localiser bar begins to swing
into the centre and the 146 turns on to final
approach under the guidance of the autopilot.
At eight miles the Glidepath indication comes
in and the aircraft begins to descend.

Captain Burns calls for the first stage of flap
and the undercarriage and Cliff complies,
calling out as each indication is received. A
call to ATC:

First Officer: 'Dan-Air eight four six is
established, descending on the Glideslope.'
Flesland Radar: 'Eight four six contact Tower
on one one nine decimal one.'

Call acknowledged and a quick change of
frequency.

First Officer: 'Flesland Tower, Dan-Air eight
four six on finals at seven miles.'
Flesland Tower: 'Eight four six continue
approach, report at the outer marker.'

Another stage of flap is called for and the
speed stabilises at 140kt. As the outer marker
is passed four miles from touchdown, the
aircraft breaks out of the cloud layer and the
runway is in sight directly ahead. The airfield

is perilously situated on a rocky peninsula
between a couple of fjords and stands out as a
cleared area surrounded by pine woods.

First Officer: 'Eight four six is passing the
marker.'
Flesland Tower: 'Eight four six is cleared to
land. Wind is two five zero degrees at eight
knots.'

The autopilot is disconnected in order to fly
the aircraft manually for landing, and speed is
further reduced by a combination of the
remaining flap stages and the airbrake. Target
threshold speed of 112kt is easily achieved and
the 146 is flared on to Bergen's undulating
runway: 'Spoilers! Ground idle!' Steady but
firm braking, and the 146 rumbles past two
taxiways and slows enough to take the third
turning on the left.

Flesland Tower: 'Eight four six landed at five
four. Contact Ground on one two one decimal
seven.'

Cliff changes the frequency and calls Ground
while the Captain completes the landing run.

First Officer: 'Flesland Ground, eight four
six.'
Flesland Ground: 'Eight four six, report
runway vacated. Park on Stand Two.'
First Officer: 'Roger Ground, Stand Two, and
we have vacated the runway.'

The after-landing checks are completed as the
aircraft taxies in to the main apron stretching
along the front of the airport terminal

building. Swinging right through 90°, Captain Burns picks up the Ground Marshaller who guides the aircraft to a stop just below the tall control tower building.

As soon as the engines are shut down, the doors are opened and the steps wheeled into position. First on board is the representative from Braathens who arranges for the passengers to disembark and provides the crew with a list of the passenger and freight loads for the next flight. The basic calculations of the fuel requirements for the next two legs, through Stavanger to Newcastle, have already been worked out before departure from Newcastle. 3,880kg will be required for the Stavanger to Newcastle flight and another 1,000kg will be used during the 20min sector to Stavanger from Bergen, making a total requirement of almost 5,000kg which is the figure agreed upon. There are 2,400kg remaining on board from the inbound flight and therefore a further 2,600kg are required.

The turnaround at Bergen is very tightly scheduled as there is a lot to be done in the 40min allowed. All passengers are disembarked as the aircraft is to be refuelled, but some will reboard for the flight to Stavanger and will be joined by new passengers flying from Bergen to Newcastle. In fact the loading of the aircraft on this leg can be very critical because the combination of passengers for various destinations means that the aircraft can be filled to capacity as well as carrying a full fuel load. In view of the small amount of

Top:
'Mike November' taxies towards Stand 2 against a backdrop of the mountains to the west of the airfield.

Above:
The musical instruments, which were such a problem to stow aboard, are unloaded at Bergen.

Below:
The First Officer checks that the refuelling is being correctly carried out.

fuel burnt off on the short flight to Stavanger, the aircraft could arrive there at a weight in excess of the maximum landing weight. On such occasions the solution is either to offload passengers or freight, or else take on less fuel and uplift more at Stavanger. Today, the southbound passenger load is 53 plus one infant, and the total payload is 4,943kg including baggage. Take-off weight will be just over 33,000kg, so the reference card is flipped over to this figure.

Cliff leaves the flightdeck after the passengers have disembarked and goes to carry out an external check of the aircraft. The baggage is being offloaded, and while checking the brakes for any signs of overheating the refuelling bowser arrives. He watches while the fuel lines are connected and, having advised the total fuel required, continues with his walk around the 146. As soon as the refuelling is completed he checks the amounts and signs the receipt for the refuelling operator.

Back on the flightdeck the crew complete the load sheet while the passengers are boarding. There is just time to snatch a bite of the crew lunch, a compact version of the meal served to passengers, but most is left uneaten for the moment. The Braathens representative has brought copies of the latest weather reports which show that the weather is deteriorating at Stavanger. It is now raining heavily there and the cloud base is down to 700ft. With the paperwork completed and all passengers on

board, the aircraft is ready to go, but there is a short delay as there is no tractor available for the pushback. This is a busy time of day at Bergen and there are several SAS DC-9s on the apron along with a Braathens F28, all making demands on the ground services.

After a couple of minutes a tractor appears and the driver gives a cheery wave before hitching up. The First Officer, who will be flying the next two sectors, calls the Ground Controller for clearance to push back and start. This is given and 'Mike November' begins to move at 1230, 5min behind schedule (the local time at Bergen is 1430). As soon as the start is completed Captain Burns calls ATC:

Captain: 'Flesland Ground, Dan-Air eight four six is ready to taxi.'
Flesland Ground: 'Eight four six taxi to the holding point for Runway one eight. OKLAN one alpha departure for Sola. Squawk four two seven six.'

This is acknowledged and read back as Cliff starts taxying northwards from the apron and along the parallel taxiway to the holding point just short of the northern end of the runway. The OKLAN Departure (SID) is a straightforward climbout on a track of 176° Sola VOR, initially climbing to Flight Level 70 and then further as instructed by ATC. Requested cruising level is 150.

As the aircraft taxies, ATC instructs the crew to change to the Tower frequency, 119.1MHz. This is done and the Captain checks in:

Captain: 'Flesland Tower, eight four six is approaching the holding point.'
Flesland Tower: 'Dan-Air eight four six, line up Runway one eight. You are cleared for take-off. Wind is two four zero at one zero knots.'

Cliff lines the 146 up on the runway, completes the pre-take-off actions and calls for take-off power. The Captain moves the thrust levers forward and, as the engines spool up, Cliff releases the brakes and the aircraft rolls forward. Eighty knots, VR (115kt) and V2 (128kt) are called by the Captain as Cliff eases the control column back and quickly establishes a 2,000ft/min climb; flaps and undercarriage are retracted and the autopilot engaged. As the aircraft passes 1,000ft it is enveloped in a thick cloud layer which persists for the rest of the flight. Fortunately, the navigation on this leg is most straightforward. Sola VOR is selected on NAV1 while Flesland

ENBR

Trans alt **4000**						G4	49

1. Min gradient 5% (300'/nm) to 4000, inform ATC if unable to comply.
2. Initial climb to FL70 if no other level specified, and expect further climb within FLE 25d. Climb to en-route cruising level will be issued by Flesland App or Stavanger Control after take-off.

	EFF
	13 FEB 86

G/S kt	100	130	160	190	220	250	
ft/min	500	650	800	950	1100	1250	300'/nm

NOT TO SCALE

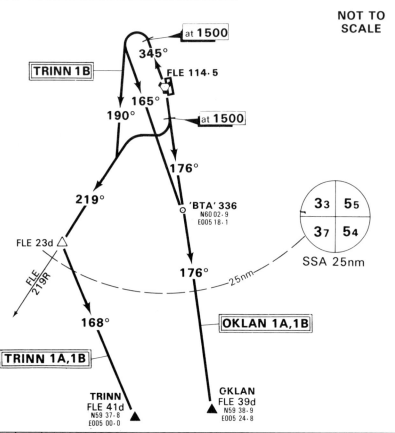

at **1500**

345°

TRINN 1B

FLE 114·5

165°

190°

at **1500**

176°

219°

'BTA' 336
N60 02·9
E005 18·1

33	55
37	54

SSA 25nm

FLE 23d △

FLE 219R

176°

—25nm—

168°

OKLAN 1A, 1B

TRINN 1A, 1B

TRINN
FLE 41d
N59 37·8
E005 00·0

OKLAN
FLE 39d
N59 38·9
E005 24·8

SID	R/W	ROUTEING (including Min Noise Routeing)	ALTITUDES
OKLAN 1A	18	Ahead on Tr 176M to OKLAN.	To FL70
OKLAN 1B	36	Ahead on Tr 345M to 1500. Left on Tr 165M to BTA then Tr 176M ('BTA'356M) to OKLAN.	
TRINN 1A	18	Ahead to 1500. Right to intercept and follow FLE 219R to FLE 23d. At FLE 23d turn left and follow Tr 168M to TRINN.	
TRINN 1B	36	Ahead on Tr 345M to 1500. Left on Tr 190M to intercept and follow FLE 219R. At FLE 23d turn left and follow Tr 168M to TRINN.	

Departure chart showing the OKLAN procedure. *AERAD*

B

British airways

AERAD ©

Rev: Notes

VOR is retained on NAV2. The flight is simply a straight leg between these two aids and the signal from Sola is quickly picked up as the aircraft climbs.

Flesland Tower: 'Dan-Air eight four six airborne at three five. Contact Flesland Radar on one two one decimal zero.'

This is done and contact established.

Captain: 'Flesland Radar eight four six is passing four thousand feet.'
Flesland Radar: 'Dan-Air eight four six continue climb to Flight Level one five zero.'

While this exchange is in progress, the First Officer switches to 126.0MHz on his VHF box and listens to the ATIS:

Sola ATIS: '. . . Sola Information Papa at one two two zero. ILS Runway One Eight. Transition Level five five. One nine zero at one one knots, seven kilometres, rain, two OKTAS seven zero zero, six OKTA one two zero zero, temperature one four, dew point one two, QNH one zero one zero . . .'

The weather at Stavanger is worse than that experienced at Bergen but is well within limits for an ILS approach. The Stavanger ILS frequency, 110.3MHz, is selected on NAV2 in place of the Flesland VOR which is no longer required.

Seven minutes after take-off, DA846 is approaching the cruising level of 150 and is instructed to contact Sola Radar on 119.4MHz:

Captain: 'Sola Radar, Dan-Air eight four six is levelling at one five zero.'
Sola Radar: 'Roger eight four six, maintain one five zero, report ready for descent.'

While the aircraft is in level flight, the First Officer makes a brief announcement to the passengers, giving them the expected time of landing and the weather conditions at Stavanger. By the time that he has done this it is almost time to start descent, with 45 miles to run to Sola showing on the DME.

Captain: 'Sola Radar, Dan-Air eight four six ready for descent.'
Sola Radar: 'Eight four six, set QNH one zero one zero, descend to four thousand feet, report ILS established.'
First Officer: 'Eight four six leaving one five zero for four thousand.'

Above:
Approaching V1 (115kt) during the take-off run from Bergen.

In fact the direct track from Bergen has brought the aircraft straight on to the ILS for Runway 18 at Stavanger as both runways are in line with each other. The Localiser bar shows that the 146 is on the centreline but the Glideslope indications are slightly high. The First Officer adjusts the rate of descent, throttling right back to 41% N1, 67% N2 and a fuel flow of 210kg/hr, and sets the autopilot to the GLS mode for the approach. As the descent is commenced, a stewardess looks in to confirm the cabin secured for landing, a straightforward check this time as no food or drinks have been served on this short flight.

Below:
Twenty-seven miles out from Stavanger: the ILS is selected on both NAV sets and power is being reduced.

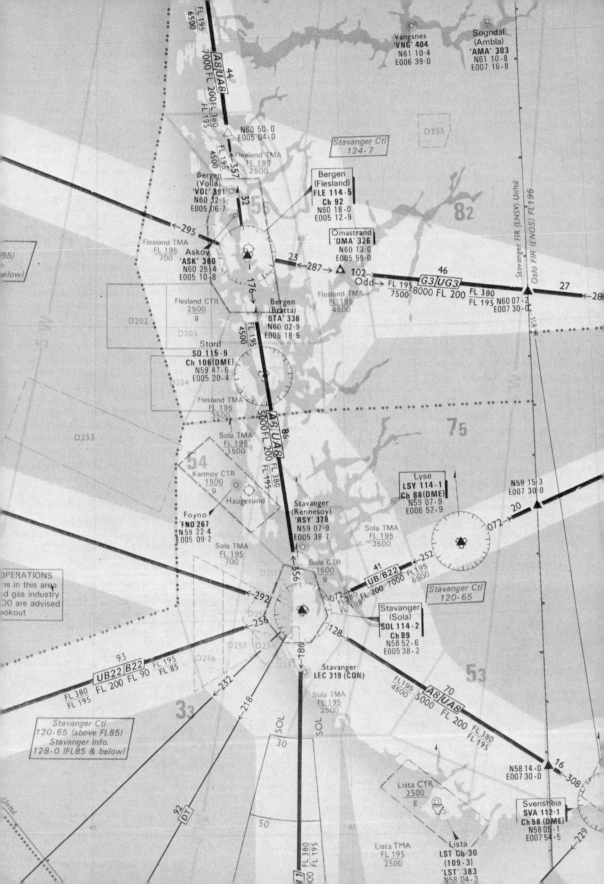

At 20 miles to run, altitude is 6,300ft and the aircraft is established on both Localiser and Glideslope.

Captain: 'Dan-Air eight four six is established.'

Sola Radar: 'Eight four six continue approach. Contact Sola Tower on one one eight decimal three five.'

The new frequency is selected and another call made:

Captain: 'Sola Tower, Dan-Air eight four six is established ILS at one six miles.'

Sola Tower: 'Dan-Air eight four six, continue approach, report at the outer marker, QFE one zero zero nine.'

The descent and approach checks have been completed by this time and both pilots check their altimeter settings, Cliff using QFE for landing while the Captain retains the QNH setting. The approach follows the familiar pattern: speed is already down to 230kt at 12 miles, decreasing to 200kt at 7.5 miles and thereafter to the threshold figure of 112kt. Similarly, the first stage of flaps come down at 6.5 miles and the rest in stages to full flap at 2.5 miles. At 1255 the 146 is crossing the outer marker at four miles from touchdown:

Captain: 'Dan-Air eight four six is passing the marker.'

Sola Tower: 'Eight four six is cleared to land. Wind two zero zero at one two knots.'

At this point the ground is still obscured by cloud and does not become visible until passing 600ft on final approach at two miles from touchdown. It is raining heavily and the wipers are quickly switched on although they have little effect on the sheet of water washing across the windscreen.

Like Bergen, Stavanger is built on a pensinula almost surrounded by water and the final approach is entirely over water except for the last couple of hundred yards. Once on the ground, Cliff brakes gently as there is plenty of runway ahead and he does not want to run the risk of aquaplaning on the wet runway surface. The aircraft comes down to taxying speed about three-quarters of the way down the runway, while the after-landing checks are quickly completed.

Sola Tower: 'Eight four six landed at five six, turn right on to Runway Two Niner, contact Ground on one two one decimal seven.'

Stavanger has two runways, 18/36 which lies north-south and has been used for the landing, and 29/11 which lies almost at right angles. There is also a complex system of taxiways and dispersals as the airfield is an operational military base which is made available for civil use. There is little for the casual observer to see as most of the military aircraft are dispersed in the woods and rock shelters which surround the airfield.

Captain: 'Sola Ground, eight four six has vacated Runway One Eight.'

Sola Ground: 'Eight four six turn right on taxiway Golf One for the main apron, follow the Marshaller for parking next to the Friendship.'

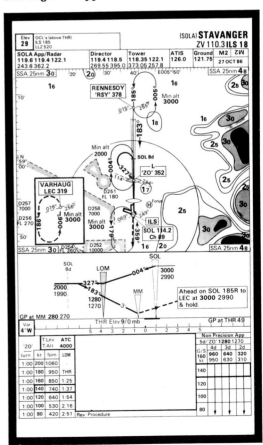

Left:
Visibility is poor and the wipers are switched on to clear the rain from the screen as the airfield comes into sight.

Below:
A marshaller guides the BAe146 into position next to a Busy Bee Friendship; the control tower is in the background.

Turning on to the taxiway indicated, the civil terminal is straight ahead. An untidy looking building, it is due to be replaced by a much larger, purpose-designed terminal which can be seen under construction to the left; this should be open in a couple of years time. The Marshaller is picked out and Cliff follows his bat signals coming to rest between a Busy Bee F27 Friendship and a SAS DC-9. The latter has landed just ahead of DA846 and is disembarking its passengers. Handling here is also by Braathens and their Dispatcher comes out to the aircraft to pick up the load sheet and escort the passengers for Stavanger to the terminal.

Having landed at 1256, after a 21min flight from Bergen, the time is now 1301 (1501 local time) and scheduled departure for Newcastle is 1315. The normal time for turnaround at Stavanger is only 20min and, with the 846 running slightly late, this tight schedule is trimmed even further. However, the procedure here is simpler than in Bergen: passengers in transit to Newcastle remain on board while those for Stavanger disembark. More passengers for Newcastle are waiting at the departure gate in the terminal building to be conducted out to the aircraft; their baggage is already being brought out for loading in the holds as soon as the Stavanger-bound items have been offloaded. The aircraft does not need refuelling and the required meal and bar stocks have been taken on board at Bergen.

In the pouring rain, Cliff carries out the normal external checks but he is pleased to be quickly back in his seat on the flightdeck. There is some delay before the passengers arrive as the ground staff seem fully occupied with the SAS DC-9 alongside. This gives an opportunity to finish off a packet of biscuits left over from the snack meal at Bergen while checking over the departure procedures from Stavanger. Using Runway 18, the laid-down

procedure for a DOLFI 1A SID is to climb straight ahead until three miles south of the Sola VOR (which is situated on the airfield), before turning right on to a heading of 285°. This heading is then maintained until the 257° radial from the VOR is intercepted, whereupon a left turn is made to follow this track to the DOLFI intersection, 28 miles out. Initial climb will be to Flight Level 70 and then as directed by ATC.

While the crew are thus occupied, a call to the Dispatcher on her radio handset advises that the passengers are on their way and final numbers are confirmed. In fact, the aircraft will be almost full with a total of 79 passengers (plus one infant); with freight and just over 4,000kg of fuel the take-off weight is 34,194kg. Landing weight is therefore calculated at 31,594kg after a total fuel-burn en route of 2,600kg.

The load sheet is completed and the various copies distributed. The First Officer calls Stavanger Ground on 121.75MHz for clearance to pushback and start, and this is given. Pre-start checks are completed as the doors are shut and the steps removed, and Chris gives the signal to the Ground Engineer to start moving the aircraft back. The time is 1230 and the start is quickly completed. With the tractor and Engineer in sight and moving away to the right, Chris calls for taxi clearance.

Captain: 'Stavanger Ground, Dan-Air eight four six is ready to taxi.'
Stavanger Ground: 'Dan-Air eight four six, taxi to the holding point for Runway one eight, QNH one zero one zero.'

As the 146 moves forward and turns right, the First Officer begins his pre-take-off checks and calls for 18° of flap. To get into position for take-off it is necessary to cross Runway 18 to the west side of the airfield, and then turn north along taxiway C1 to reach the end of the runway. Initially, there is a short wait on the edge of the apron while the SAS DC-9, which has already taxied out, is cleared for take-off. As it passes in front from left to right, Ground Control calls again:

Sola Ground: 'Dan-Air eight four six, cross the runway.'
Captain: 'Eight four six Roger, entering the runway.'
Sola Ground: 'Eight four six, it will be a DOLFI one alpha departure for Newcastle, Squawk four two seven six. Contact Tower on one one eight decimal three five.'

The First Officer acknowledges this clearance, which is expected, and checks that the navigation aids are set up as required for this. Sola VOR (114.2MHz) is set up on NAV1 while the ILS for Runway 18 is on NAV2 in case it should be necessary to return after take-off for any reason. On reaching the end of the taxiway, the pre-take-off checks have been completed.

Captain: 'Tower, Dan-Air eight four six is ready for take-off.'
Sola Tower: 'Dan-Air eight four six is cleared for take-off. Wind is one nine zero at one five knots.'

With the wipers switched on to full to clear the heavy rain from the screen, take-off power is selected and brakes released. The 146 moves smartly forward, the Captain calling out the speeds, and Cliff lifts it off at 1331. The undercarriage is retracted and almost immediately the aircraft is enveloped in the low cloud. 'Flaps up' is called as 700ft is passed in the climb.

Below:
Passengers embark at Stavanger, eager to get out of the pouring rain.

Sola Tower: 'Dan-Air eight four six, airborne at three one, contact Radar one one nine decimal six.'

Captain Burns selects the frequency and calls up:

Captain: 'Sola Radar, Dan-Air eight four six turning right.'
Sola Radar: 'Dan-Air eight four six continue climb to Flight Level one five zero.'
Captain: 'Eight four six to one five zero, request direct routeing to Newcastle.'

There is a short pause before Radar reply:

Sola Radar: 'Eight four six cleared direct Newcastle.'

The DOLFI SID is intended for aircraft routeing on Airway Upper Blue 22 which is the direct track from Stavanger to Aberdeen. A direct route to Newcastle diverges by some 25° to the south of this and so it was necessary to obtain ATC clearance to diverge from the SID procedure and pick up the 232° radial from the Sola VOR.

The 146 maintains a rate of climb of 2,000ft/min and the engine instruments show N1 at 90.4%, N2 at 92%, TGT at 800°C and fuel flow at a rate of 850kg/hr. Four minutes after take-off, the aircraft is already passing 8,000ft and Sola Radar come up with further climb instructions:

Above:
Lining up for take-off, the Captain selects the engine anti-icing 'on'.

Right:
Departure tracks from Stavanger. *AERAD*

Sola Radar: 'Dan-Air eight four six continue climb to Flight Level two eight zero. Contact Stavanger Control on one two zero decimal six five.'

The 146 has now been cleared all the way up to the requested cruising level and the Captain changes frequency as instructed. At this stage the aircraft is still in the thick cloud layer but at 1338 it breaks out into bright sunshine as Flight Level 130 is passed. Another 10min passes before Flight Level 280 is reached, when Cliff levels off and reduces power to the cruise settings (N1 87%, N2 89%, TGT 755°C, fuel flow 500kg/hr/engine).

As soon as this has been done, the DME readout shows that the aircraft is 90 miles out from the Sola VOR and is therefore crossing the Stavanger/Scottish FIR boundary.

Captain: 'Stavanger, Dan-Air eight four six is the FIR boundary at four eight, Level at two eight zero '
Stavanger Control: 'Roger eight four six, contact Scottish Control on one three five decimal eight five.'

ENZV

Trans alt **4000**								G1	ＬＧ

1. Initial climb to FL70 if no other level is specified. Expect further climb within SOL 25d. Climb to en-route level will be issued by Sola Approach or Stavanger Control after take off.

EFF 13 FEB 86

2. Min gradient R/W's 18/36 5%(300'/nm) to 3000ft, if unable to comply inform ATC.
3. Approach will issue enroute cruising levels to controlled IFR flight after take off.

G/S kt	100	130	160	190	220	250	
ft/min	500	650	800	950	1100	1250	300'/nm

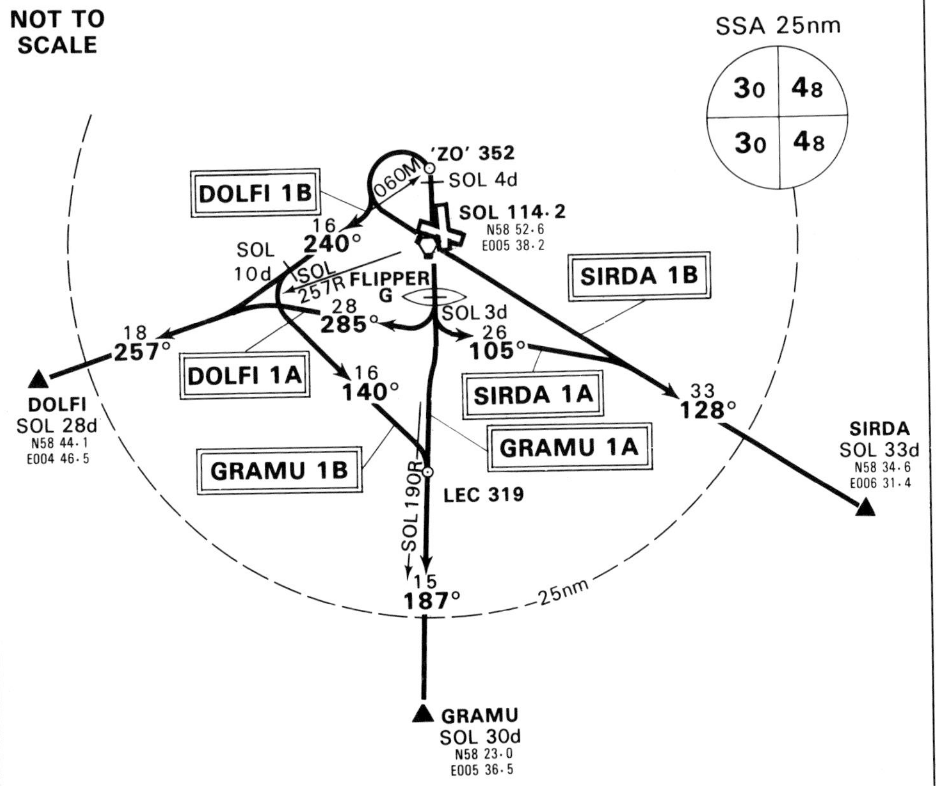

NOT TO SCALE

SSA 25nm

3o	4 8
3o	4 8

'ZO' 352
SOL 4d
DOLFI 1B
060M
SOL 114·2
N58 52·6
E005 38·2
16
SOL **240°**
10d SOL
257R FLIPPER
G
SOL 3d
SIRDA 1B
18 28
257° 285°
26
105°
DOLFI 1A
16
140°
33
128°
DOLFI
SOL 28d
N58 44·1
E004 46·5
SIRDA 1A
GRAMU 1A
GRAMU 1B
SOL 190R
LEC 319
SIRDA
SOL 33d
N58 34·6
E006 31·4
15
187°
—25nm

GRAMU
SOL 30d
N58 23·0
E005 36·5

	SID	R/W	ROUTEING (including Min Noise Routeing)	ALTITUDES
B	SIRDA 1A	18	Ahead to SOL 3d,then left onto Tr 105M then right to intercept and follow SOL 128R to SIRDA.	To FL70
	SIRDA 1B	36	Ahead to SOL 4d then left to SOL.At SOL intercept and follow SOL 128R to SIRDA.	
	GRAMU 1A	18	Ahead on SOL 187R to GRAMU.	
	GRAMU 1B	36	Ahead to SOL 4d,then left onto Tr 240M ('ZO'060M).At SOL 10d left onto Tr 140M (LEC 140M) until crossing SOL 190R,then right to intercept and follow SOL 187R to GRAMU.	
	DOLFI 1A	18	Ahead to SOL 3d,then right onto Tr 285M then left to intercept and follow SOL 257R to DOLFI.	
	DOLFI 1B	36	Ahead to SOL 4d,then left onto Tr 240M ('ZO' 060M),then right to intercept and follow SOL 257R to DOLFI.	

AERAD British airways

© Revision: Initial climb notes.

This call is acknowledged, Captain Burns changes frequency and checks in, reporting his position and level, and also advising that the ETA for Newcastle is 1432 (which will be 1532 BST). Once established in the cruise, the flightdeck routine continues. The First Officer has a word with the passengers and then tunes in to the VOLMET to obtain the latest Newcastle weather report. This gives a westerly surface wind at 14kt, visibility more than 10km, six Oktas cloud cover at 2,000ft, temperature 17°C and QNH 1,020. As a matter of routine he also checks the reports for Edinburgh and Manchester which show similar conditions.

At 1353, with the aircraft now some 130 miles out from Stavanger and 220 miles to go to Newcastle, ATC call with another frequency change:

Scottish Control: 'Dan-Air eight four six Squawk one four zero six and contact Border Radar on one three four decimal eight five.'

The Captain changes frequency and calls:

Captain: 'Border Radar, Dan-Air eight four six Level at two eight zero. Newcastle at three two.'
Border Radar: 'Roger eight four six, maintain two eight zero, Squawk Ident.'

There is a few seconds' pause while the Controller watches for the identification on his radar and he then calls back:

Border Radar: 'Eight four six identified at two two zero miles northeast of Newcastle. Runway two five is in use. Report ready for descent.'

Already the Newcastle VOR frequency (113.5MHz) has been selected on NAV1 and within a few minutes it is picking up a strong signal and shows 199 miles to run. The next 10min are reasonably quiet and the crew relax over a coffee while checking the fuel figures. By now the passengers will have finished their light meal and the cabin staff will be doing the rounds with duty-free goods before starting to clear the cabin for landing.

At 1410, with 120 miles to go, the First Officer calls Dan-Air Operations at Newcastle to confirm the aircraft's arrival time and passenger load. With this report made, it is time to prepare for the descent and approach to Newcastle. The ILS frequency, 111.5MHz, is set on NAV1 and Newcastle VOR transferred to NAV2. With 99 miles to run, Captain Burns calls for descent clearance:

Captain: 'Border Radar, Dan-Air eight four six is ready for descent.'
Border Radar: 'Dan-Air eight four six, descend to Flight Level one zero zero.'

This is acknowledged and the power settings adjusted to give a 1,500ft/min rate of descent. The First Officer has another word with the passengers to inform them that the aircraft is starting descent and should be landing within 20min. This also serves as a warning to the cabin crew who can be hard-pushed on a short flight like this. In just over an hour, they have to serve a meal with wine and coffee, clear away the empty trays, run a bar service, sell the duty-free goods and then clear and secure the cabin for landing. If the flight is shortened by a strong tailwind, the last few minutes can be quite hectic!

As the aircraft leaves its cruising level at 1412, a check shows that a total of 1,500kg of fuel has been used since take-off. The rest of the descent checks are carried out and at 1424 the aircraft is 45 miles out from Newcastle and passing Flight Level 115. There is little cloud over the sea, but a build-up of cumulus clouds can be seen ahead over the coast. Another call from Border Radar:

Border Radar: 'Dan-Air eight four six, Squawk seven two four zero, contact Newcastle Radar one two six decimal three five.'

While the Captain acknowledges the call and changes frequency, the First Officer reaches down and sets the new code on the Transponder.

First Officer: 'Newcastle Radar, Dan-Air eight four six is four four miles on the zero five one radial, passing Level one one zero, Squawking seven two four zero.'
Newcastle Radar: 'Roger eight four six, Squawk Ident, continue descent to Flight Level six zero, radar vectoring for Runway two five.'

The Autopilot Altitude Selector is wound down to 6,000ft and Chris presses the Ident button.

Newcastle Radar: 'Eight four six is identified at four zero miles northeast of Newcastle. Current weather is two seven zero at one five knots, visibility two five kilometres, six Okta two thousand feet, QNH one zero two zero, QFE Runway two five one zero one zero, temperature one eight.'

Captain Burns acknowledges this and reads back the pressure settings and, for the

Left:
The English coast in sight, although clouds are obscuring the airfield which lies some 15 miles ahead.

Below:
Two-mile final for landing on Runway 25.

moment, continues on a heading of 230° direct to the Newcastle VOR. The time is now 1527.

Newcastle Radar: 'Dan-Air eight four six, report your heading.'
Captain: 'Eight four six heading two three zero.'
Newcastle Radar: 'Eight four six turn left heading two two zero, descend to three five zero zero feet on QNH one zero two zero.'

The aircraft is now passing Flight Level 65 and the approach checks continue. APU is selected 'on', both altimeters set on QNH and the cabin seat belt sign illuminated. The cabin is reported as secure for landing as ATC call again.

Newcastle Radar: 'Dan-Air eight four six is one eight miles from touchdown, closing the ILS from right to left, report established.'

Although the coastline is now in sight, the cloud layer is covering the airfield and so both pilots monitor the ILS indications as the range decreases. At 13 miles from touchdown, the autopilot starts a turn to the right at the Localiser beam comes in. By now the aircraft is level at 3,500ft, speed is being reduced, and is just below the Glidepath.

Captain: 'Eight four six is Localiser established.'
Newcastle Radar: 'Eight four six is cleared ILS approach. QFE threshold one zero one zero.'

The First Officer sets the QFE on his altimeter and waits for the descent to start as the autopilot locks on to the Glidepath. As it does so he calls for the first stage of flap. At eight miles to go, the aircraft is crossing the coast and is now below the cloud layer. The airfield is in sight straight ahead.

Captain: 'Dan-Air eight four six is at eight miles with the field in sight.'

Above:
**'Eight four six is cleared to land. Wind two six
zero at one four knots.'**

Newcastle Radar: 'Eight four six continue
approach, contact Tower on one one nine
decimal seven.'

The Captain changes frequency as requested
and at the same time calls for the undercarriage and then 24° of flap. A rumbling noise
and three green lights confirm that the wheels
are down as he checks in with the Tower:

Captain: 'Tower, Dan-Air eight four six is at
six miles.'
Newcastle Tower: 'Eight four six is cleared to
land. Wind two six zero at one four knots.'

Cliff now disconnects the autopilot and
continues to fly the aircraft manually. As he
approaches the runway, he calls for the
remaining flap and uses the airbrakes to
achieve his threshold target speed of 112kt.
The touchdown is good and with spoilers out,

engines set to ground idle, he brakes firmly to
slow up in time to take the turning on the right
for the main apron. The time is 1434 (1534 BST
at Newcastle) only 4min behind the scheduled
time of arrival.

The Tower breaks in with taxying
instructions and directs DA846 to park on
Stand 3. At the same time DA843 from Oslo can
be heard checking in at eight miles on the ILS.
This flight is also on time and, once on the
ground, will be picking up passengers from
DA846 who are travelling on to Manchester.

Once clear of the runway, the crew run
through the after-landing checks, retracting
the spoilers, flaps and airbrake as they taxi
towards the parking stand where the
groundstaff are waiting to unload the passengers and baggage, and to prepare the aircraft
for its next flight. The aircraft is brought to a
standstill, engines shut down, and the doors
opened as the final checks are completed. With
all passengers disembarked, paperwork completed and the cockpit tidied up, the crew are
ready to leave after briefing the Engineer on
the state of the aircraft. This is the end of their
duty period for today, although occasionally it
would be necessary to stay with the aircraft

Above:
Flaps and spoilers are retracted as DA846 taxies off the runway.

Right:
Shutdown — the throttles are brought right back to the ground idle position. Lifting the catch at the rear of each lever will enable it to be brought fully back to the fuel cut-off position. On the left is the lever for operating the airbrake and spoilers.

for two further sectors, to Gatwick and return. Today, this is not necessary and Captain Burns and his First Officer are able to walk across the apron in the warm afternoon sunshine as the third crew of the day are arriving at the airport to prepare for the next flight. The aircraft's working day is still only half complete!

Evening and Night

After arrival from Stavanger, there is approximately an hour-and-a-half on the ground at Newcastle before 'Mike November' is airborne again at 1600 (1700 BST) for Gatwick. The schedule calls for an 'on chocks' time of 1710 at Gatwick, followed by a departure at 1750 for the return to Newcastle where it should arrive at 1900 (2000 BST). The south and northbound flights are designated DA107 and DA108 respectively and the Captain this evening is Les Bates. Together with his First Officer, he will have arrived at the airport at around 1500 in time to carry out the pre-flight planning before checking out the aircraft, the procedure being identical to that carried out by the crew of the early morning DA101.

This evening's flight is well patronised with 75 passengers on board and Captain Bates achieves an on-time departure, pushing back at 1559 and getting airborne at 1606. The flight to Gatwick is uneventful and follows the pattern set earlier in the day. Landing time is 1658 and a few minutes later the aircraft is parked again on Stand 6 by the domestic pier.

The returning DA108 is fully booked with 86 passengers on board, many of whom will be businessmen who will have travelled down to London on the morning flight. With the day's work successfully completed, they will be looking forward to a relaxing flight and a three-course dinner with wine and coffee, as well as complimentary drinks from the bar. Definitely better than the train!

At 1752, less than one hour after landing, the aircraft is pushing back and starting. Runway in use is still 25 and a Daventry SID is again given for departure. However, as Captain Bates lines up on the runway there is a minor incident which illustrates the pressures on the single runway at Gatwick. A Boeing 757 which has just landed ahead is instructed by the Tower to turn off the runway at taxiway Delta which is almost at the far end. However, the pilot starts to take the turn-off before Delta, the one which is notified as being closed for repair work. Although he is warned by the Controller, the pilot has to stop the aircraft and then turn round in the taxiway entrance before continuing down the runway to the correct turn-off. By this time there is a Dan-Air Boeing 737 on a 2-mile final to land. The Controller now has to act quickly to avoid a 'go around' by the 737 and orders DA108 to pull forward and clear the runway to the right on taxiway Bravo. Captain Bates moves the 146 smartly forward for 300m to reach the taxiway and turns off as instructed. In the meantime the 757 is just clearing the runway at the far end and the Controller can now clear the 737 to land. With the excitement over, DA108 is cleared to continue back along the taxiway and line up again.

This time the departure, at 1803, is uneventful and the Captain changes to Gatwick Radar as he turns right after take-off. By this time in the evening the traffic levels in the London TMA are fairly light and the Controller gives immediate climb to Flight Level 120 on a heading of 060°. On changing to London Control on 128.4MHz, the controller requests best rate of climb to Level 120 and turns the aircraft left on to a heading of 015° which brings it straight through the TMA, passing directly over Heathrow. Only too pleased with this time-saving route, Captain Bates selects full climb power and achieves over 4,000ft/min. Once past Heathrow, further climb to cruising level is quickly given and also a direct routeing to the Pole Hill VOR which is passed at 1834, only 31min after take-off.

SCHED	819	SP		1825	AMS	1900
73 34	819	SP		2005	MME	2025
T		SP		2045	NCL	
8x846		14				
GATES	107	MN			NCL	1600
88 47	108	SP		1710	LGW	1750
SCHED		SP		1900	NCL	
				✱ C I P		

From there, a direct track to Newcastle, followed by a visual approach leads to a landing at 1849 (1949 BST), a total flight time of only 46min. After landing, the aircraft is directed to Stand 9 on the domestic side of the pier for parking. By 1905, all the passengers have left the aircraft and the crew are tidying up and collecting their bags before handing the aircraft over to the engineers.

Normally the engineers would have the aircraft for the night in order to carry out routine checks and rectify any unserviceabilities which may have built up during the day. However, today being a Friday, there is only a two-and-a-half hour period available to them as the aircraft is scheduled to make a positioning flight to Tees-side Airport at 2130 in order to make a 2300 departure from there for Palma.

The crew for these flights will be Captain John Waddingham and First Officer Ron Swann, whose duty period starts at 2030 when they arrive at Newcastle Airport to start the flight planning procedure. Although the main sector originates from Tees-side, all the weather information for the flight is provided by Newcastle. As the passenger figures for the flight have not as yet been notified, it is assumed that it will be full and planning for fuel and weights proceeds on that basis.

The weather reports and forecasts are very favourable due to an area of high pressure over France and Spain. At 30,000ft the upper winds are westerly at 50kt for the first half of the route, but becoming southwesterly at 80kt over southern France and Spain. There is a warning of possible turbulence over southern France in the lee of the Pyrenees.

The flight from Tees-side to Palma should take 2hr 45min giving a fuel requirement, including reserves, of 7,600kg. In addition, another 600kg is needed for the short flight to Tees-side which is 31 miles to the south of Newcastle, so the aircraft needs to carry a total of 8,200kg. After checking that ATC hold all the relevant flight plans for the three sectors, the pilots collect their bags and walk out to the aircraft parked beneath the terminal building on Stand 9.

The Engineers are still working on the aircraft and are attempting a wheel-change on the port main undercarriage. Using a small hydraulic jack, the port wheels have been raised off the ground while attempts are made to remove the outer wheel which is stubbornly jammed on the stub axle. Leaving the Engineers to struggle on, the Captain starts his cockpit checks while the First Officer does an external check of the aircraft and supervises the refuelling but, with these tasks completed, the wheel-change has still not been completed. The crew therefore have no option but to sit and wait as the engineers work away, occasionally calling for the brakes to be applied or released. Eventually the problem is solved, the new wheel fitted, and the jack lowered.

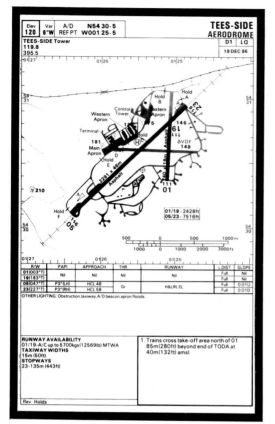

Elev 120	Var 6°W	A/D REF PT	N54 30·5 W001 25·5	TEES-SIDE AERODROME

TEES-SIDE Tower
119.8
395.5

D1 LQ
18 DEC 86

01/19 - 2428ft
05/23 - 7516ft

R/W	PAPI	APPROACH	THR	RUNWAY	L.DIST	SLOPE
01(003°T)	Nil	Nil	Nil	Nil	Full	Nil
19(183°T)	Nil				Full	Nil
05(047°T)	P3°(LH)	HCL 4B	Gr	H&LRL EL	Full	0.01U
23(227°T)	P3°(RH)	HCL 5B			Full	0.01D

OTHER LIGHTING: Obstruction, taxiway, A/D beacon, apron floods.

RUNWAY AVAILABILITY
01/19-A/C up to 5700kgs(12569lb) MTWA
TAXIWAY WIDTHS
15m (50ft)
STOPWAYS
23-135m (443ft)

1. Trains cross take-off area north of 01 85m(280ft) beyond end of TODA at 40m(132ft) amsl.

Rev: Holds

Left:

Tees-side Airport layout. The three runways betray the military origins of the airfield, known as Middleton St George when it was an operational RAF station. *AERAD*

congestion at the busy destination airfields. A Friday night in August is obviously one of the traffic peak periods and DA2852 from Tees-side to Palma has therefore been allocated a departure time of 2308. Failure to make this 'slot' time could result in several hours delay before another slot is available; with the late arrival of the aircraft, the pressure is on to complete the turnaround as soon as possible. Consequently, the cabin crew embark as soon as the doors are opened and commence the loading of the meals and the duty-free bar stocks. Ground handling at Tees-side is by British Midland Airlines who pull out all the stops to ensure that the aircraft meets the departure time.

While the cabin is being prepared, the Captain goes over the load sheet with the Dispatcher. As with most holiday charter flights at this time of year, the aircraft has an almost full load of 86 passengers plus one infant and, with fuel already uplifted, the total ramp weight is 37,300kg. This is less than 1,000kg under the maximum permitted take-off weight. In fact this flight is one of the longest undertaken by Dan-Air's BAe146 fleet; the longest of all, also operated from Tees-side, is to Alicante on the Spanish mainland.

By 2250 the aircraft is ready and the passengers, who have completed check-in formalities some time before, are led out from the terminal for boarding. By 2300 they are all on board, the steps pulled away and doors closed. With a few minutes to spare, John Waddingham talks to the passengers on the cabin PA system and welcomes them on board, describing the route which the aircraft will follow tonight. This will take it across the Channel, down the western side of France, over the northeast of Spain and the Mediter-ranean to the destination in the Balearic Islands.

At 2303 John initiates start-up and calls for taxi clearance. The parking arrangements at Tees-side mean that a pushback is not required and the aircraft can taxi directly off stand. There is a short backtrack before lining up on Runway 24 and, having been cleared for take-off, the brakes are released at exactly 2308. The high aircraft weight leads to higher take-off speeds and Ron calls VR at 123kt and V2 at 135kt. Gear up at 140kt and then speed is allowed to build up to 180kt before retracting the flaps. The TMS is set to the TGT mode with

There is no cabin crew aboard the aircraft at the moment as they are based at Tees-side and will embark on arrival there. When the steps are withdrawn, the First Officer therefore goes back to the cabin to close the doors and ensure that the evacuation chutes are set to deploy automatically. As soon as this is done he returns to the flightdeck and the Captain calls the Tower for start-up clearance, using the callsign 'Dan-Air two eight five two papa' (the 'papa' suffix indicates that this is a positioning flight).

Start-up clearance is given and pushback commences at 2215 (2315 BST), more than 30min late. The flight to Tees-side is straight-forward, the time en route being only 8min and cruising level only 3,500ft. It is a clear night and the airport is in sight from several miles out so John elects to make a visual approach to Runway 24 and by 2232 the aircraft is parked on the apron in front of the terminal departure lounge.

Flights from the UK to the popular Mediter-ranean holiday resorts are subject to Air Traffic Flow Management (ATFM) procedures which are designed to ensure an even flow of traffic across southern Europe and to prevent a temperature of 830°C selected which gives N1 at 93.5% and fuel flow of 720kg/hr/engine. A few minutes after take-off Tees-side call with an Airways Joining Clearance:

Tees-side Approach: 'Dan-Air two eight five two cleared via Ribel and Upper Amber two five to Palma, join Controlled Airspace five miles east of Ribel climbing to Flight Level two nine zero. Squawk five five seven zero.'

This clearance is acknowledged and, at 2313, the aircraft is instructed to contact London Control on 128.05MHz. The controller on the Pole Hill sector clears DA2852 to route direct to the Barton VOR and the climb continues. It is a very clear night and, as the aircraft turns south on to Airway Amber 25 after crossing Barton, the lights of Liverpool shine brightly just below on the right while over on the left is the sprawling Manchester conurbation. The cities show up as areas of misty white light liberally crossed with strings of amber pinpoints marking the major roads with their sodium street lights. These sights are pointed out to the passengers by the First Officer as the 146 passes through Flight Level 230 while, in the meantime, the Captain listens in to the London Volmet to get an update on the latest UK weather reports. This is a formality as virtually everybody is CAVOK (literally 'Ceiling and Visibility OK') which means that the visibility is greater than 10km and there is no cloud below 5,000ft. He also takes the opportunity to call Dan-Air Operations at Gatwick to report that the flight was airborne on time and to pass the passenger load and ETA for Palma (0145).

At Flight Level 290, 20 minutes after take-off John levels off the 146 and adjusts power for the cruise. On reporting his level to London, he is directed to take up a heading of 190°, obviously to keep clear of a Britannia Airways 737 which can be heard on frequency heading north and descending into Manchester. In cruising configuration, N1 is 92%, N2 is 90% and TGT is 772°C which gives an IAS of 250kt, equating to a TAS of 382kt.

After a few minutes the heading restriction is cancelled and John turns on to a heading of 197° to route direct to the Berry Head VOR on the south Devon coast. This is crossed at 2353, at which point London pass the aircraft to Brest Control on frequency 135.65MHz. With relatively light traffic on the Airway, the French controller clears the aircraft to route direct to the COGNAC VOR which is 280 miles ahead, avoiding a slight zigzag in the normal route which would have crossed the Dinard

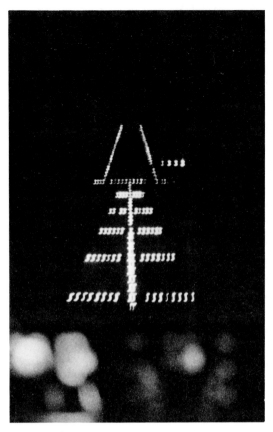

Above:
The approach and runway lights for Runway 23 at Tees-side. The bar of four lights to the right of the runway edge provides an indication to the pilot in respect of his height on the approach.

and Nantes VORs. The Captain sets a heading of 162° on the autopilot and monitors the aircraft's position by reference to VOR/DME readouts from the various VORs. In addition, while over the sea, he switches the radar to the mapping mode and can see the outline of the French coast ahead. Passing over Guernsey and Jersey, the 146 crosses the Brittany coast over Dinard at 0012 (0112 BST on Saturday morning). The Cognac VOR is coming in strongly now and shows 166 miles to run, making the navigation fairly straightforward.

In the meantime, John has tuned into the Barcelona Volmet transmissions to pick up the latest weather reports for the Spanish airports. The Palma weather at midnight is given as wind calm, visibility 6km in mist, two oktas at 2,000ft, temperature is 23°C and the dew point 22°C — obviously warm and very humid.

Still on Airway Upper Amber 25, the aircraft heads steadily south and crosses the Cognac

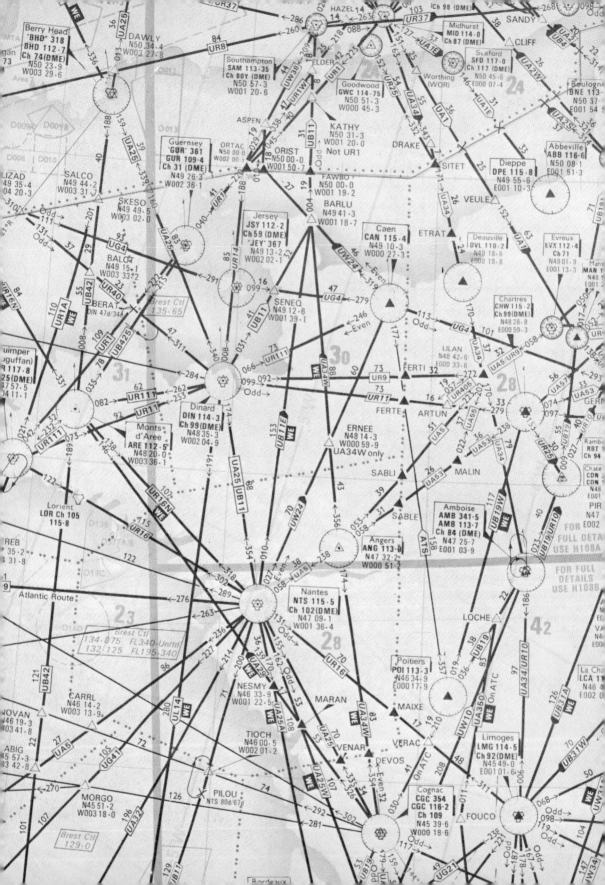

Right:
The weather radar can also be used in the mapping mode. This shows the French coast at Dinard 40 miles ahead while the Cherbourg peninsula is to the left. The Channel Islands would be almost below but do not show as the radar beam is not depressed enough to pick them up.

Left:
Part of the complex system of airways over northern and western France: DA2852 follows Upper Amber 25 and 25 West. *AERAD*

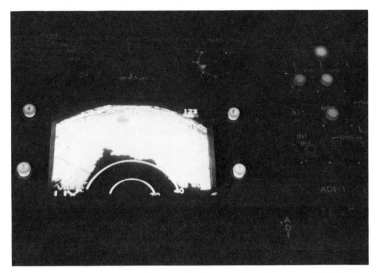

VOR at 0030 and is then cleared direct to the Toulouse VOR 140 miles away on a track of 155°. As John turns on to the new heading, control of the aircraft is transferred to Bordeaux ATCC on frequency 134.00MHz.

The Captain now takes the opportunity to run over the fuel figures. At 0140 a total of 3,750kg has been used since start-up and there are 1,900kg left in each of the two wing tanks. The landing weight will be just over 31,000kg and so he selects this figure on the reference card to display the landing speeds. Planning ahead, he also does the calculations for the return flight to Tees-side and notes that 7,580kg will be needed.

At this stage of the flight, the passengers will have finished their meal and most will be having a short nap before landing. However, in contrast to the earlier flights in the day when most of the passengers have been flying on business, there is a definite holiday atmosphere on board. Many passengers, particularly some of the children, have asked if they can visit the flightdeck. As things are relatively quiet during the long cruise over France, the Captain is happy to allow this and for a while there is a steady stream of children (and their dads) to marvel at the arrays of instruments and controls while the pilots try to explain in simple terms what is happening.

While these visits are in progress, the Toulouse VOR is passed at 0101 and the Captain turns right on to a track of 182°, heading towards Barcelona. At 0107 the Franco-Spanish border is crossed at reporting point Estat, 59 miles DME from Toulouse, and control is transferred to Barcelona ATCC on 132.05MHz who advise that Runway 24 Right is in use at Palma. Shortly after this John turns

left on to a heading of 155° on course for the Barcelona VOR. By now some turbulence is being experienced, as expected from the route forecast, so the cabin seat belt sign is switched on and cabin staff ensure that the passengers are secure in their seats. Speed is reduced to Mach 0.6 (235kt IAS) and eventually descent to a lower level is requested. This is approved by the Barcelona Controller who clears the aircraft down to Flight Level 240 as it approaches the Barcelona VOR. The latter is crossed at 0124 and a left turn is made on to a new heading of 168° for the last leg of the flight to Palma which is now only 116 miles ahead.

Once over the Mediterranean the turbulence dies down and speed is increased to 250kt. John now contacts Dan-Air Operations at

Below:
At night the appearance of the cockpit is altered by the discreet lighting.

Palma and informs them of the ETA and passenger load, and also the fuel uplift required for the return flight. The company maintain their own operations section at Palma due to the large number of flights scheduled into Palma during the summer season. In turn they are able to advise that the outbound load will be a full one, 88 passengers plus one infant, and payload of 7,333kg. The maximum allowable is 7,500kg.

When some 30 miles southwest of Barcelona, control is transferred to Palma Approach on 121.3MHz. As the First Officer reports approaching Flight Level 210, Palma gives further descent to Level 100 and confirms that it will be a procedural ILS approach to Runway 24 Right. This means that instead of being guided by radar on to final approach for the runway, the pilots will be expected to follow the ILS procedure as laid down on the instrument approach chart.

At the moment NAV1 is set on the Mike Juliet Victor (MJV) VOR which is just south of the airfield, but once over the island it should be possible to pick up the Papa Alpha (PA) NDB which is the starting point for the ILS procedure and is four miles out on the runway centreline.

Palma Approach now instruct the DA2852 to Squawk 7333 and to continue descent to Flight Level 70, direct to the PA. This is the lowest altitude they can allocate in this sector due to the mountains rising to almost 6,000ft on the north side of the island. Levelling off at 70, there is still five miles to run to the beacon and the crew have visual contact with the airfield. However, in view of the high ground surrounding the approach, it is deemed safer to continue with the ILS procedure until established on final approach. Crossing the PA at 0142, John turns left on to the outbound heading of 061° and begins descent to 2,700ft, bringing the thrust levers right back to give a 2,000ft/min descent rate. The approach checks have already been completed and when 10 miles east of the airfield a left turn on to a heading of 270° is commenced to bring the aircraft on to a closing heading with the

Localiser track. Once steady on this heading, the aircraft is passing 3,500ft and speed has been reduced to 160kt. Flaps and undercarriage are selected and the airfield lights are now clearly in sight ahead as the autopilot locks on to the Localiser.

A change to the Tower frequency, 118.3MHz, and landing clearance is given. Surface wind is calm and John now flies the aircraft manually for the landing. At four miles the Glidepath pointer is centred and power is increased to reduce the rate of descent to 700ft/min. Full flap comes down at three miles, speed drops to 110kt over the threshold and a slight jar signals arrival on the runway.

Over to the left is the apron and terminal building complex with over 20 other aircraft immediately in view. Leaving the runway on taxiway Foxtrot, the crew complete the after-landing checks and look ahead to see a van with an illuminated 'Follow Me' sign moving in front. Palma Tower confirm that there are no delays for the departing flight (DA2853) and instruct the 146 to follow the van to the parking stand. This takes the aircraft between the ranks of parked airliners and

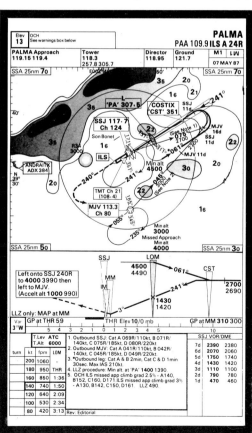

Left:
The final stage of the route crosses the Toulouse and Barcelona VORs, then over the Mediterranean to Palma at bottom right.
AERAD

Right:
ILS procedure for Runway 24 Right at Palma. Coming from the north, DA2852 will route to the PA from the northwest before turning left to go outbound in the descent. *AERAD*

round to the northeast apron where a Marshaller directs it on to Stand 5.

As soon as the engines are shut down, the usual fleet of service vehicles closes in, the doors are opened and the steps positioned. The warm night air is humid and oppressive; without the air conditioning on, the main cabin becomes uncomfortable as the passengers disembark and are taken by two articulated coaches to the terminal.

Approximately one hour is allowed for the turnaround at Palma and the crew receive a substantial meal prepared on the ground at Palma. This is taken in the main cabin where both pilots can relax for a while with the cabin staff, while a party of cleaners bustle through the cabin chattering happily in Spanish. Halfway through the meal, the refuelling bowser arrives and Ron interrupts his eating to check that the correct amount is loaded. He finishes off his meal later while the Captain does an external inspection of the aircraft.

By 0230 the aircraft has been refuelled and is ready for the passengers to embark. The Dispatcher passes this information on by radio and is advised that the first coachload is on its way. The crew quickly clear away their meal trays and the pilots return to the flightdeck to prepare for start-up. With a full load it takes a while for everybody to embark and settle in their seats and so it is 0248 before Ron, who will be flying the return leg, calls the Tower for start-up clearance. The interior of the aircraft is dripping condensation due to the high humidity and temperature, but once the engines are running the air conditioning can get to work and conditions slowly improve.

Top:
The BAe146 sits under the floodlights at Palma surrounded by fuel bowsers, catering vehicles, baggage trolleys and vans.

Above:
While the cabin crew take a break, the cleaners work through the rows of seats.

As DA2853 taxies for Runway 24, the Tower passes the departure clearance which specifies a Drago One Alpha departure. This involves a climb straight ahead until passing 1,500ft before turning right to cross the ADX NDB at 3,000ft or above, and then following the 317° radial direct to the Maella VOR; the latter is some 87 miles west of Barcelona. Once on track, the aircraft will maintain Flight Level 60 until further cleared to climb by ATC.

Airborne at 0256, Ron turns right after passing 1,500ft, picking up the 295° radial from the MJV VOR, and calls Palma Approach on 121.3MHz. Further climb to Flight Level 150 is given and 112.1MHz is set on NAV1 to pick up the Maella VOR, now 131 miles away. Twenty-four miles out from the MJV, Palma Approach clear the aircraft to continue climb to Flight Level 240 and shortly afterwards transfer control to Barcelona. Climb power settings are N1 95%, N2 93%, TGT 840°C and fuel flow 900kg/hr.

After passing Maella, the route home follows Airway Upper Amber 34 West to the Tarbes VOR in the south of France, and then over Bordeaux and up the western side of France, across the Channel to Berry Head and thence to Tees-side. This routeing is designed to avoid confliction with the southbound flow of traffic over central France during busy periods, but adds considerable extra mileage. As traffic seems quiet, the Captain asks for a more direct route, but after deliberation the Barcelona Controller refuses this and directs the aircraft to continue via Maella. This is crossed at 0324 by which time clearance to Flight Level 280 has been given and the 146 has levelled off in the cruise.

Turning north on to a track of 005° for the Tarbes VOR, control is eventually transferred to Bordeaux as the aircraft approaches the border at point Perdu (38 miles south of Tarbes). The French Controller is more forthcoming than his Spanish counterpart and clears DA2853 direct to Barlu. This is a point on the north French coast at Cherbourg and means that the aircraft can now follow the track of Upper Amber 34 West all the way across France, using the VORs at Sauveterre, Cognac and Angers. Tarbes is crossed at 0348 and the crew settle down to clear up some of the routine tasks. The technical log is brought up to date and all charts, except those needed to complete the flight, are filed away in their folders. At 0400 a check on the fuel shows that 2,800kg have been consumed and there are 2,450kg in each of the wing tanks, plenty to complete the flight as planned.

On the port side the lights of Bordeaux can be seen, with the Gironde Estuary faintly visible. Looking to the east a red glow is beginning to colour the distant sky, signalling the coming dawn. The Cognac VOR is passed at 0410 and this is the point at which control is transferred to Brest on 134.875MHz (one of the recently allocated frequencies based on a 25kHz channel separation).

Ten minutes later Ron is able to pick the London Volmet transmissions and check on some of the UK weather reports. These are mostly good, although some of the southern airfields are reporting mist patches with visibility only 2,000m in some cases. The Tees-side weather is not on the Volmet transmission.

The 146 cruises on through the gradually lightening dawn. Most of the passengers are asleep, having been up most of the night, and the cabin is quiet. By the time Barlu on the north French coast is crossed at 0450, it is light enough to make out the coastline; the sky to the east is reflecting the yellow of the rising sun. Ron is now in touch with London Control on 134.45MHz and is cleared to route to the Sampton (Southampton) VOR and then direct to Pole Hill for Tees-side. Over the Channel, Ron calls Dan-Air Operations at Gatwick giving the flight details and ETA at Tees-side. A call to London FIR on 124.75MHz obtains a copy of the Tees-side weather which is CAVOK with a temperature of 11°C.

After passing Sampton the flight continues heading north, skirting well to the west of the London TMA and crossing Upper Amber 1 at Honiley. At this point, the Captain asks London (now on 128.05MHz) for a direct routeing to Tees-side and this is approved. He turns on to a heading of 003° and when 60 miles south of the Pole Hill VOR requests clearance to commence descent. London approve descent to Flight Level 180 and the power is reduced slightly to leave the cruising level.

It is now full daylight and the east coast with the Wash and the Humber Estuary show up well on the right. At 0526 the aircraft is approaching Flight Level 180 when London advise that descent may be continued to Flight Level 60 at the Tango Delta (TD) NDB which is the main radio beacon at Tees-side and is used for the ILS procedure on Runway 23. A few minutes later the 146 passes through Airway Blue 1, 22 miles east of Pole Hill and, as soon as it is clear of this, London passes instructions to contact Tees-side Approach on 118.5MHz.

Switching frequencies, John calls up and is cleared to the TD at 2,500ft on QNH setting 1023mb for a procedural ILS approach to Runway 23. The weather is confirmed as CAVOK with the surface wind calm and, after a quick discussion, the crew ask for a visual approach to Runway 05 which will save time due to the shorter mileage involved. This is approved by Tees-side Approach and both pilots look out for the airfield, now some 20 miles ahead. Eventually the runway comes into sight and Ron leaves 3,500ft to commence his approach. As the speed drops below 200kt he lowers the undercarriage and then selects 18° of flap. The landing checks are quickly run through and he sets the QFE (1,018mb) on his

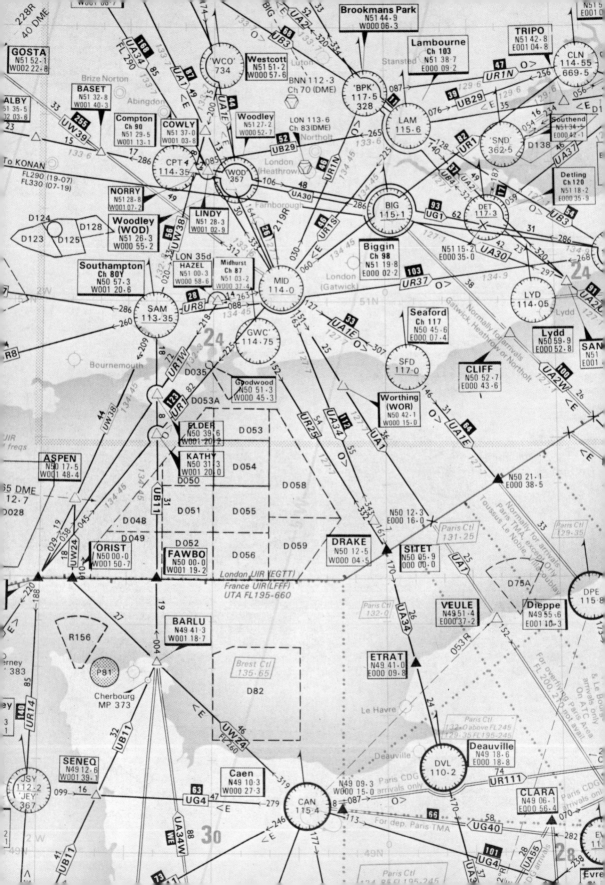

altimeter. As the speed decreases, the rest of the flap is lowered in stages; when the aircraft is turned on to final approach it is two miles from touchdown passing 600ft at 120kt. A quick application of the airbrake on short final brings the speed right back and Ron flares firmly on to the runway, quickly braking to make the runway intersection turn-off for the apron.

Landing time is 0542 (0642 BST), and a few minutes later the aircraft is on the apron with the passengers disembarking. All power is shut down including the APU in the tail (electrical power being supplied by a GPU standing by the nose), and the crew disembark. After checking and signing the accounts for the bar and duty-free goods sales, the Captain says goodbye to the cabin crew (who live in the Tees-side area) and, with his First Officer, makes his way out of the terminal. Here they pick up a waiting taxi which will take them the 40 miles by road back to Newcastle Airport where their duty period began almost 12hr previously. Both pilots sleep during the ride and the driver knows better than to attempt conversation!

For the BAe146, 'Mike November', there is little rest: within an hour a new crew will be arriving to fly another return trip to Palma and this will be followed by an overnight flight to Venice. On the Sunday there will be flights to Jersey and Alicante before returning to Newcastle overnight, ready to operate the scheduled service to Gatwick on the Monday morning. The aeroplane, after all, is only a machine and needs no rest . . .

Left:
A high level chart showing northern France, the Channel and southern England. The aircraft is routeing via Upper Amber 34 West to BARLU, thence to Southampton and almost due north towards Pole Hill. *AERAD*

Below:
Turning final for a visual approach to Runway 05 at Tees-side. In the half-light of the morning the details of the airfield can just be made out.

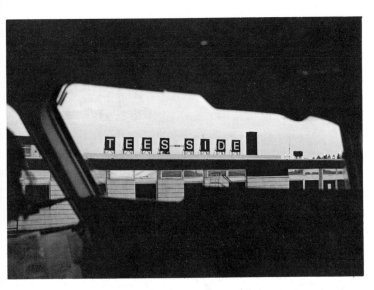

Far left, top:
... Ron flares firmly on to the runway...

Far left, bottom:
... quickly braking to make the turn-off for the apron.

Left:
'Ah yes! this looks like the right place!'

Below:
The passengers disembark, perhaps unaware that the landing they have just made is the tenth by this aircraft in the last 24hr. While they, and the crew, will be looking forward to a rest after the flight, the BAe146 will soon be airborne again ...

Overleaf:
The BAe146 sports clamshell airbrakes at the rear of the fuselage. These are highly effective in adjusting speed and rate of descent on final approach.

... DAWN